D1135151

VALLE-INCLÁN

CENTENNIAL STUDIES

A Fernando Alegría, con la de encontrarle en Austin, y un gran abrazo de Ricardo Gullón

VALLE-INCLÁN, *Photograph by* ALFONSO, *Madrid*

Valle-Inclán

VALLE-INCLAN
CENTENNIAL STUDIES

Edited by
RICARDO GULLÓN

Cover design by
CRISTINO MALLO

THE UNIVERSITY OF TEXAS
DEPARTMENT OF SPANISH AND PORTUGUESE
Austin, Texas
1968

Library of Congress Catalog Card Number: 68–65410

COPYRIGHT © 1968 BY BOARD OF REGENTS,
THE UNIVERSITY OF TEXAS AT AUSTIN

CONTENTS

FOREWORD

Don Ramón del Valle-Inclán (1866–1936), born in Villanueva de Arosa, in the extreme Western part of Spain, a land of mystery, was not only one of the greatest writers in the Spanish language in this century but at the same time the creator and protagonist of his own legend. Novelist, dramatist and poet, he traced with sure strokes the outlines of a mythical figure which turned out to be his own.

In Galicia, where he was born, there still persist deeply-rooted folk beliefs of a magical and mythical character, of extremely remote—probably Celtic—origin. Attracted by these beliefs, Valle-Inclán wrote stories in which fantastic creatures move hand in hand with ordinary ones and become confused with them. Witches, the *Santa Compaña,* or walking phalanx of lost souls, the Devil himself, appear in novels or dramas which, although not realistic, do not thereby fail to seem real.

Midway through his life Valle-Inclán changed, and with him his style. He viewed the world and literature from a different perspective, or perhaps simply with new eyes, and he found no sense in what he saw: the stupidity, the cruelty and the misery which made up his world—and ours. So it was that his theater has been considered a theater of the absurd, *avant la lettre.* The tragic and the grotesque, mixed in unequal doses, caused him to see life as a drama either grotesquely tragic or tragically grotesque. He was not the first to make this discovery, but it was he who came up with an expressive term to define the literary genre in which those ingredients were manifestly employed. *Esperpentos* was his name for those dramas and novels in which the heroes appear systematically deformed, as though seen in the concave mirrors into which man occasionally peers, to see himself as the ridiculous image which the glass reflects for him. Because of this deformation he was called an anti-realist by those who refused to accept the idea that man may be a caricature of himself and that very caricature an expression of a disquieting but indisputable truth.

Another great Spanish writer, Miguel de Unamuno, said that Valle-Inclán's most important invention was perhaps his language, in some instances a mixture of Spanish and Hispanic American speech, and throughout most of his work a singularly personal creation, impregnated with folk elements and neologisms, and animated by images at once original and efficient.

From that perspective and with that language Valle-Inclán produced an extensive and important series of works in which critics customarily discern two or three different epochs. Although this is possible, perhaps the initial and intermediate stages are really no more than moments of an evolution which is to culminate in the *esperpento* and in the dissolute and degraded view of the world underlying this type of invention.

The Department of Romance Languages of the University of Texas, wishing to take part in the centennial celebration of the birth of Ramón del Valle-Inclán, organized a series of lectures relating to the life and work of the writer. These lectures are reproduced here, together with an essay written by me as an epilogue to the tribute.

For their assistance I should like to thank the Chairman of the Department, Theodore Andersson and the members of the organizing committee: Luis A. Arocena, George D. Schade, Douglass Rogers, Humberto López-Morales and Virginia Higginbotham, and most especially Pablo Beltrán de Heredia, the designer of the present volume, as of the program announcements, and Miguel González-Gerth, the secretary of the committee. Thanks are also due to Douglass Rogers and José Sánchez for their translations of the lectures of Ildefonso Manuel Gil and José Luis Cano, respectively; I acknowledge further my gratitude to James Anderson and Lucy Costen for her aid in the preparation of the manuscripts and to Sergio D. Elizondo for his collaboration as director of a dramatic reading of *Romance de lobos* in which teachers and students of the Department participated. My cordial thanks to all of them.

RICARDO GULLÓN

RAMÓN MARTÍNEZ-LÓPEZ

A PORTRAIT OF VALLE-INCLÁN

Translated by

MIGUEL GONZÁLEZ-GERTH

The recollections of Don Ramón del Valle-Inclán I share with you here cannot begin to give a true picture of the man. The most to which I can aspire is to draw a vague, impressionistic profile, since my personal acquaintance with the writer was belated and rather sketchy. Yet I hope that my remarks will contribute, in some small measure, to the restatement of the much debated though no less beguiling problem of his real personality. I have thought that to coordinate my reminiscences with some of the more obvious and recurring traits of his works might prove to be helpful. Thus I shall endeavor to establish a relation between Valle-Inclán's life and his work, without impairing the autonomy which each should retain. Despite its partial truth and the ingenuity it demonstrates, the notion that Valle-Inclán became a mask of himself or one of his own literary characters, and even worse, the suggestion that, like Dr. Frankenstein, he was the victim of his personal creation, can easily lead us astray. I sometimes detect in such a point of view the reflection that Valle-Inclán's own style has cast upon his biographers and critics. Consider, for example, what he wrote in his *Lámpara maravillosa,* a work not sufficiently studied: "I have over my face a hundred fictional masks which follow one another under the miserly rule of a fate without transcendence." He adds: "Perhaps my true face has not yet been revealed, perhaps it never can be, under so many veils hoarded by the days and woven by the hours. Not even I know myself and perhaps I am doomed never to know."

An approach which does not take into account all the evidence will be wrong for one of two reasons: because it will be based either on an erroneous perspective between the biographer and his subject or on the excessive reduction of the whole personality to one of its significant facets. Just as a diamond cannot be appreciated through one of its glimmers, neither can a human life be assessed through a few acts no matter how noble. If we are to grasp the whole man that was Valle-Inclán, it will not be through what Azorín correctly termed his "extrinsic tumult"; that is, whatever the outer man kept from his inner self, or through so many anecdotes, either true or false, which have been adduced as valuable biographical documents. On the other hand, it appears that not enough has been thought about what the great writer did with his mask, his alter ego. That part of the man which nourished Unamuno's paradoxical spirit, in Valle-Inclán always had a cohesive function, both aesthetically and ethically. Let us not make the mistake of accepting literally the definition of *esperpento* given by Max Estrella in *Luces de Bohemia.* "The *Esperpento* is produced by the reflection of classic heroes in concave mirrors. The tragic sense of Spanish life can only be expressed by means of a systematic deformation of aesthetic values." This *systematic deformation* does not derive from the mirrors on the Calle del Gato but from Valle-Inclán's talent for satire and humor, as had been the case with Quevedo and Goya. In a memorable essay, Pedro Salinas has outlined the development of the *esperpento* which began long before Max Estrella gave it a name. The mask of Spanish society presents itself, almost at the very beginning of Valle-Inclán's works, as a profound yet artistically vague protest which was not at all alien to the spirit of the Generation of '98. Whether in Valle-Inclán's time or ours, Spain does not have to be held up to a concave mirror in order to appear as "a grotesque deformation of European civilization." The deformation is merely the result of a painful comparison.

This beaten path leads neither to the art nor to the personality of Valle-Inclán. It is another matter to attempt, by means of definite recollections, to authenticate Valle's biography and to determine its correlation with the themes and stylistic features most consistently found in his works.

In the life and works of Valle-Inclán there are always two distinguishable levels of half-fiction, half-reality, more or less related and sometimes even fused; at one level, what is narrated in his works or suggested by his life; and at the other, the meaningful experiences he, whether acting as author or simply as a man, tries to communicate to his contemporaries. As a prerequisite to the penetration of these levels, Valle-Inclán demands the intelligent and sensitive cooperation of his readers; he would have them constantly aware that beyond this mixture of fiction and reality there is an expression (of long tradition in Spanish literature) of an uncompromised ethical content. The last thing Valle wanted to do, however, was to construct a fixed body of ideas and concepts. He guarded himself against criticism in this respect by stating in his Modernist manifesto of 1902: "Ideas have never been the exclusive property of those who expound them. They exist and develop in the realm of intellect. The most the writer can hope to do is to perpetuate them through the infusion of his personality or the beauty of his expression." "Personality" and "beauty of expression," in this context, are equivalent terms.

One of Valle's greatest accomplishments is that he was able to bring together aesthetics and ethics into a superior artistic vision. His art, like all great art, is born precisely of this determination *not* to separate the man or his works from the world that surrounds them. Thus the presence of Valle-Inclán in his writings, the intervention of his self-image in the characters he created, is not surprising. The *Sonatas* have the collective title of *Memoirs* not only because it recalls those of Casanova but because it refers to a literary genre which lends itself to the projection of the author into his work and, in this case, into his central characters. Ildefonso Manuel Gil, in the study included in this volume has drawn attention to a whole series of "innocent victims" in the works of Valle-Inclán, presenting them as undeniable proof of a sentimental symbiosis. He writes: "In the case of the characters in question, we see not only the varying degrees of compassion the author shows toward the individual victims, but also the reiterated protests against the brutality of some, the indifference of others." Guillermo Díaz-Plaja, who has published one of the most important and provocative books on Valle-Inclán, speaks of a process of "gradual approach" to the here and now. This process barely perceptible in the *Sonatas* and in the *Comedias Bárbaras* and *Flor de Santidad*—these last two works suggest a medieval setting—, becomes more and more evident as the author deals increasingly with situations drawn from the historical present, as for example in *El Ruedo Ibérico, Luces de Bohemia,* and the *Esperpentos.* This observation can be methodologically useful in the study of Valle-Inclán's works, but it must be stressed that, where any great author is concerned, the means of expression used to carry out this process never follows a logical plan. The question of fantasy and reality, and their interaction, is one of the most complex and far-reaching in modern literary criticism. The public has never failed to become emotionally involved in Cervantes' *Numancia* simply because its action takes place two thousand years ago. The Spanish drama of the Golden Age thrilled theater-goers of the 17th century with its Visigothic and medieval kings and heroes.

The many aspects of reality to which Valle-Inclán reacts in different ways and to various degress are seen from aesthetic perspectives afforded him, on the one hand, by his fondness for the past with its knights, servants, bastard offspring and beggars, and on the other by his hostility toward contemporary social norms. This dichotomy is artistically justified by the writer. It does not follow, however, that from his position of emotional and personal detachment, he is converted into a mere spectator who can ignore the reality of the worlds he contemplates. García Pelayo, in a brilliant essay "On the social world in Valle-Inclán's works," (*Revista de Occidente,* Nos. 44–45) says, concerning the duality in Valle's artistic behavior:

> With regard to Spanish society, Valle-Inclán's works disclose an attitude of *engagement* and of partiality, the latter of which, here, must not be understood as something negative. For the very situation of friendship or enmity, love or hate, often allows one to discover qualities in objects that remain hidden to the more neutral eye.

It would be totally wrong to believe that Valle's stylistic subtleties made him no more than an admirable master of form. On the contrary, it might be appropriate to ask, without trying to ascribe to him a concrete revolutionary ideology, whether the presence of a strict aesthetic discipline does not in itself imply an equally clear ethical standard. The artist will always appear in his singularity, with differentiating characteristics owing more to his creativity than to his volition. This is no paradox. It opens the way to a better interpretation of the well-known "mask theory" as a legitimate instrument for what has been called the *artistic control of the imagination* as *imaginative theorizing.* It takes the form of a type of syllogism, one of whose premises has been voluntarily omitted in order to arrive more quickly at the conclusion. One illustration of this key process is found in an interview which took place in 1926. As Valle said:

> Spain is like a coin. It has two sides; one is Roman, the other Moorish. Spain went to America as a child of Rome but also took along her Islamic character. Now the recent military campaigns in Morocco on behalf of the dictatorship of Primo de Rivera, are evidence of the fact that we are returning to Moorish barbarity. We must turn the coin over and try to live according to our Roman heritage.

Beneath such surprisingly simplistic historical notions there is the desire to lead Spain toward the fulfillment of her true destiny by opposing to the questionable African ventures the ideals of classical civilization.

His own native province he curiously divided between what he called Hellenic Galicia and the other which he considered characterized by *cursilería celtoide* (Celtic bad taste). And to the Ría de Arosa, near which he was born, he gave the name *Tirreno* in the preface to a book by his friend García Martí.

> I am linked to García Martí by very strong bonds which are the result of a spiritual community derived from contemplating the same native landscape and knowing the same type of people. Love and grief, singing and weeping by this blue sea with dolphins, laurels and tendrils, the Thyrrhenian sea of Arosa.

I first met Valle-Inclán in the spring of 1929, thanks to a letter of introduction from my father and the personal intervention of Fernando González, my fellow competitor for a professorship and an already established poet. In the back of a café known as the Granja del Henar, Valle-Inclán was holding one of his *tertulias.* Among the faithful participants were Manuel Azaña, Enrique Díez-Canedo, Luis Bello, Luis García Bilbao, Cipriano Rivas Cherif, Juan José Domenchina, Francisco Vighi, Honorato de Castro, and already mentioned, Fernando González. Don Ramón, a natural exemplar of courtesy and amiability, was expounding his theories with missionary zeal and, like most good preachers would often resort to the rhetorical *ex-abrupto.* His aim was to hold his listeners spellbound. He gesticulated, with face and arm, and, as Alfonso Reyes put it, while his face expressed the dogma, his arm would round it out, as might a corollary. His meeting me reminded him of one of his notions, that of Galician Hellenism, and he expounded it with the support of delightful etymologies of his own invention.

> We from the Arosa estuary come from the best part of Galicia. The trouble is that the study of Spanish geography is in the hands of men like Dantín Cereceda who have no imagination at all. And yet it could not be more obvious. Next to the village of *Dena* lies the beach called *La Lanzada.* There can be no doubt that the names come from the goddess Diana and her spear.

A few years later, during a political crisis, Valle had the opportunity to predict which men would take over the government. He gave the names of all the future ministers save that of the Navy. Some one in the *tertulia* pointed out the omission, to which Valle replied with a knowing smile. One by one the names suggested to him by his companions were dismissed and, finally, he indirectly satisfied the growing curiosity by stating his own program for such a ministry. The make-believe program went like this:

> We must strive to build a great Atlantic fleet which will include all the merchant vessels of Spain and Spanish-America; a single navy flying a single flag and bearing a figurehead which we shall commission Macho to design

> under my supervision. Like the galleons of old, these ships will cross the Pacific from the Phillipines to the Mexican port of Acapulco and they will arrive safely in Seville, since the English are not even pirates any more . . . But, no, that will never happen, because the Minister of the Navy will be that playboy from La Coruña whose only experience has been with yachts.

This sort of imaginative theorizing when applied to his satire (and who can think of satire without a moral intent?) or to his scornful detachment from the vulgar bureaucracy of his time, from a developing bourgeoisie and from a flock of court-parasites, left its special and indelible mark on the life and work of Valle-Inclán. An outstanding example of this is his declaring himself a Carlist, a defender of a lost cause which offered nothing but the satisfaction of gallantry supporting the vanquished. How else can one explain any compatibility, political or otherwise, between Valle and the barbarous Curate of Santa Cruz? Ironically, the only royal favor he ever received was being dubbed a "knight of the order of proscribed legitimacy," a favor which Don Jaime, the Carlist pretender, rather inopportunely bestowed upon Valle a few days after the Republic was proclaimed. At that time Don Ramón was voicing his regret that the new regime had not made a revolution, with all its inevitable yet decisive violence, rather than a peaceful change in the governmental structure.

Valle also applied his imaginative theorizing to his own inflexible standards of personal integrity. Six months after being appointed Curator General of the National Art Institute, he resigned. Some friend of the Minister of Agriculture had been granted permission to hunt pheasants on the Real Sitio de la Granja (the former retreat of the Royal family). In vain did Valle-Inclán protest against such an outrage, arguing that the pheasants were a beauty of the landscape.

Back in 1920, the suppression of the 1918 strike in Asturias still fresh in people's minds, Valle had said to Rivas Cherif in an interview: "What should we engage in? Not in art. To indulge ourselves at the present time is immoral and villainous. What we must achieve is social justice."

Valle-Inclan's dignity is strikingly evident in the face of defeat as a candidate for representative from his province to the Spanish Parliament. "I have raised Galicia to the highest level of art and have neither asked for anything in return nor sunk to adultation. You, Señor Tenreiro, who can make no such claims, have demanded from her a certificate of election after resorting to means that I could never employ. This is the ethical difference between us, Señor Tenreiro."

Once again we see a confluence of aesthetics and ethics. *Tirano Banderas,* the culmination of the *esperpentos,* written under the Peninsular counterpart, is an indictment of all Spanish American military dictatorships. In a letter to Alfonso Reyes dated December 23, 1923, Valle states:

> A revolution should go all the way. The *gachupines,* who represent the very essence of Iberian savagery, own 70% of the land. When in the hands of such foreigners, the land becomes the most pernicious kind of property. [The thing to do is to] expel the *gachupines*. Better still, of course, would be to put them to the sword.

I remember Valle-Inclán during the last few months of his life. He had resigned as director of the Spanish Academy of Fine Arts in Rome and had gone back to Santiago de Compostela where he had been a student. His *tertulias* now gathered at the café called the Derby. Valle had fully rejoined his Galicia, his landscape, his people. One afternoon I walked with him along the Paseo de la Herradura as he expressed the desire to tread once more the hillside of Santa Susana that overlooks the place. "That's the solution given by Columela to these problems," he said. "One must read Columela, especially in his magnificent hexameters and not in the pedestrian 17th-century prose version."

In Santiago, Valle-Inclán wrote his last articles for *Ahora.* On October 2, 1935 (two months before his death) he published an admirable review of Manuel Azaña's *Mi rebelión en Barcelona.* It is like an omen which still moves us today:

> *Mi rebelión en Barcelona* reaches its highest aesthetic level when, soberly and without romantic overtones, it accomplishes the dramatically baroque purpose of putting us in the breathless anticipation of irreparable hazards and dangerous misfortunes. This quiet book leaves us with a last terrifying suggestion. After finishing it, the reader feels he has just visited a museum of ancient instruments of torture. The tight prose resurrects ghosts of the past which we believed had long since been abolished. It reawakens the larvae of terror inspired by judges of other times who willingly hear absurd and venal charges, by scribeners, by horn inkwells, by relators' offices, by hoods of condemned men, by criers, by hangmen, by the records of the whole judicial drama still gnawed by rats in the cellars of the old chanceries.

One afternoon Valle tries to impose his theory of salmon trout in the Ulla River on a table companion, an expert in the matter but a trivial conversationalist. Another time he talks about the historian Murguía, who fifty years earlier had prefaced one of Valle-Inclán's first books. Still another time he sings the praises of Archbishop Gelmírez, assigning to him an important place in the history of Spain. Calm and renunciation now envelope the figure of Valle-Inclán. He knows that death is near and distracts himself with new illusions. A drive is started to obtain a *pazo* (manor house) for him. He speaks of his wine cellar and of the probable thirst of the priests from the neighboring regions when they visit his "parrish." That winter Valle-Inclán is forced to go to a local hospital, never to recover. The cruel malady which consumes him inflicts unspeakable sufferings. At last the awaited moment comes, and a few minutes later I am standing by the bed where he lies, pale and motionless. The talented artist Maside draws a sketch which will be reproduced many times. On his dead lips Valle-Inclán has a smile suggesting both pain and scorn. There lay the man with the highest moral integrity of his generation.

FRANCISCO AYALA

VALLE-INCLÁN AND THE INVENTION OF CHARACTER

EL PRESIDENTE
DEL ATENEO DE MADRID

IV [illegible]

Voy en la noche de luto
la boca muda a la queja
los ojos al llanto enjutos

[illegible]

Soplo de luz afligida,
Bajo el arco de la muerte
tiembla [illegible] luz de mi vida.

Muerte bienaventurada
Toda mi esperanza [illegible]
En llegar a tu posada

Translated by

MIGUEL GONZÁLEZ-GERTH

Today, a hundred years after his birth, there are certain biographical aspects of Ramón del Valle-Inclán which have become increasingly controversial. One in particular I would like to discuss here, during the Centennial Celebration organized and sponsored by the Department of Romance Languages at the University of Texas: namely, to what extent is the writer's life significant for the understanding of his written work? Regardless of their relative truth, do the picturesque anecdotes told about him hamper the real appreciation of his artistic production? Does his fascinating personality, when seen outside the context of his literary accomplishments, draw attention away from the artistic values he sought and achieved through his pen?

The truth is that to remember Valle-Inclán, Unamuno or Baroja, whom we of this generation had the good fortune to know, to talk with occasionally or to encounter on a street in

Madrid, produces a very strange sensation. It is almost as if we could remember Cervantes, Lope de Vega or Quevedo alive. These men continue to bear down upon us with their personalities thus forcing us to regard their work as something exclusively their own, putting an end to our search, in the other direction, to find the man in his works. Their personalities are still alive in many of us. And yet, this is precisely what matters. Because of their stature as men and because of their attitude toward literature, such a group of writers does not easily recede to the background usually assigned by scholars to past authors whom they often consider mere names under which to file the titles of meaningful works. In one way or another, the writers of whom I speak were always ready to stand up and affirm their individuality. Because they wished it so, their works clearly reflected their personalities instead of these being simply the circumstancial source of what was written. Unamuno, for example, the most complex and far-reaching of the group, time and time again voiced this desire; a desire shared by the members of the so-called Generation of '98 and, moreover, one which corresponds to the true nature of their art. It is clearly manifested in the dress and other external traits adopted by the group, though in this respect only Valle-Inclán went to extremes in his determination to stand out. As Ramón Gómez de la Serna said in his biography, when Valle-Inclán first showed up in Madrid, he offered to the public eye a most conspicuous masquerade along the Calle de Alcalá. Unlike the others, he did not diminish his sartorial contrivance as the years went by; to the very end, Valle-Inclán was to cut a bizarre figure. He attracted general attention; people turned to look at him, and those who did not know him through his works knew him immediately by his appearance. This practice was, for him, more than a passing literary fashion; it stemmed from the innermost recesses of his personality. It was inseparably linked with his capacity for originating legend which, as we shall see, is the source of his literary genius.

There is, connected with the name of Valle-Inclán, a complex legend made up of many false anecdotes surrounding a core of actual deeds and sayings. The fictional elements have become fused with the historical and have thus enriched and embellished an already picturesque figure. The case of Valle-Inclán is not unique in this respect, even in Spanish literature. One should keep in mind the outstanding precedent set by Francisco de Quevedo in the 17th century. Of course, the impression made by such a legendary personality involves a serious distortion of reality, but at the same time it becomes an indespensable factor of that very reality insofar as it provides the histrionic dimension of the writer.

Valle-Inclán's theatrics have been pointed out frequently by the critics, sometimes in derogation and condemnation, other times in full recognition of their positive and profound character. For example, when Ramiro de Maeztu refers to this aspect of Valle-Inclán's personality, he does so with disdain. But Unamuno, who once expressed in an unfogettable passage of *Cómo se hace una novela* the painful suspicion of being perhaps himself only a farse, looks at Valle-Inclán's theatrics with deep understanding. In truth, such histrionics are a manifestation of his creative imagination; they have the same wellspring as his legend and his literary works.

This is precisely what those who, in embarrassment, try to cover up Valle-Inclán's public reality fail to see. They argue that his eccentricities bear no significance to his works or that perhaps they even damage them. An example of such a notion is found in the preface to an edition of selected works of Valle-Inclán by another Gómez de la Serna (not Ramón). "Valle-Inclán Past Mid-Century" opens with this statement: "Upon considering the case of Valle-Inclán in the second half of this century, it is immediately evident that Don Ramón's picturesque life has gradually ceased to spawn anecdotes while his works have gained acceptance into anthologies." It is clear that a contrast is made here between the writer's life, along with the events which constitute it, and his works. It is also insinuated that literature is something destined to anthologies. And the preface continues:

> To the Spanish reader past mid-century, the fascinating fable of Don Ramón has begun to fade, eclipsed by the unknown yet real Don Ramón and even more quickly by the pure worth of his writings. As time goes by, Don Ramón becomes more his work than the Don Ramón who existed for a few and whose rodomontades and extravagant acts, whether true or attributed, produce in the critic a certain sadness and not a little contempt.

Such statements as these betray a serious problem of definition involving the concept of literature: what relationship should exist among author, work and reader? The current trend is to disregard the author's personality, considering its function to be merely instrumental in the production of a work which is of value in itself and whose effect upon the reader is all that really matters. At the time of its conception, this approach was a healthy reaction against an exaggerated sociological and/or biographical focus in literary criticism which distracted from the appreciation of the intrinsic merits of a given work. As a reaction, there is no doubt that it was justified and worthy of praise, but it is also true that we must now recognize that this method, like any other, can be carried to extremes. The fact is that we would not be interested in the personal circumstances of a man who might have written this or that work but who actually did not. We would only be interested in the circumstances of the man who did write it. It is true, however, that a literary work is, in itself, an autonomous entity whose author can be unknown without that fact altering its significance. *Lazarillo de Tormes* is a case in point. All we know about the author and his circumstances is what we can infer from the text. This is most unfortunate because we are deprived of a great deal which might help us arrive at a better understanding, a more complete interpretation. For despite its autonomy and self-sufficiency, the work of art is the vehicle through which communication is established between the writer and his readers. Within its structure, there are meaningful elements which originated in the mind of a man; a man, as Unamuno liked to say, "of flesh and blood", endowed not only with the sensibility necessary to envision such elements but also with the ability to give them communicable form, as in the case of the poet who works with a particular verbal construction. Contained within that form, the elements will evoke analogous experiences in countless readers or listeners. But one must not forget the intent to communicate by means of a technical device and that behind this device lies the creative spirit of the artist. Readers of Cervantes cannot help being conscious of the author's own vision of the world in his works. The reader of Quevedo, on the other hand, has the feeling that what remains of the author in his work is something camouflaged. This distinguishing trait lies outside the scope of literary values, though it may well support them.

In the specific case of Valle-Inclán, his unusual personality was the source of tremendous misunderstanding. On the one hand, there were the semi-literates (including journalists), incapable of seeing beyond the picturesque surface, and, on the other, there were those who shared Maeztu's views exposed in an article published July 8, 1936 (six months after the death of Valle-Inclán):

> Valle-Inclán's personality, his work and his influence were never fused. Neither does the man have much to do with the work, nor the work with the influence it exerted. Valle-Inclán was essentially a great actor, impressive and bizarre, who used the whole world as his stage . . . The only relation between Valle-Inclán and literature was that the favorite targets of his invectives were other writers.

Surprising as it may seem, Maeztu looks upon Valle-Inclán as a man who walked the streets and frequented the cafés, who now and then locked himself in his room to write, but who ultimately had nothing to do with his own creative production. Maeztu judges from an extremely narrow point of view. According to him, Valle-Inclán's work presents a "negative aspect of the world, [it is] a ballet watched by a deaf man or religion assessed by a confirmed skeptic." Not only is he blind, as a critic to the aesthetic elements prevalent in his production, but he also fails to recognize the profound ethical content of its satire.

On the whole, it seems a mistake to separate the author from his work. There are cases, however, in which to do so bears the support of the writer's own volition, such as in the case of those who deliberately shy away from public view and draw a clear-cut line between their writings and their private lives, thus determined to exist, as it were, on two planes. So it was with Benito Pérez Galdós, the great 19th century novelist with a transparent spirit like Cervantes, who nevertheless kept his daily life a secret, as did Calderón de la Barca in the 17th century, in contrast to the effusive Lope de Vega. Of course, when the reader perceives an elusive personality behind a work of art he likes, the result is an increasing interest and the wish to lift the concealing veil. In any event, what is essential about a man is invariably revealed in his work. Even if anonymous, a work of art must be considered as having been conceived by someone of whose personal circumstances the reader just happens to be unaware.

To ignore Valle-Inclán's character in order to concentrate on his works is, in my opinion, totally absurd since personality and creation, in his case, form an inseparable whole. The title of this paper does not refer to character in general; that is the various fictional characters created by Valle-Inclán in his writing. It refers to Valle-Inclán himself as a character who does, however, often become confused with some of those who appear in his works. It is well known that in his famous "autobiography" published in *Alma Española,* he took credit for deeds which he would later attribute to his Marqués de Bradomín. And sometimes, in his own life, he exhibited attitudes and repeated phrases which he had previously assigned to his characters. Don Ramón deliberately and artfully designed an image for himself. There is no dichotomy at all between the man and his work; what he wrote began with the stylized projection of his inner self, a fact that prompted Ramón Gómez de la Serna to speak of him as being a "mask." His greatest creation was his personality from which followed his written works. Hence the legend which surrounds him.

It is not surprising that such a man would be the object of gross misunderstanding. Once again we are reminded of Quevedo. Countless persons who have never read him, or who might even be illiterate, have the impression that he was a comic, the author of frequently quoted jokes, the vast majority of which are not, nor ever could have been, his. This is an obvious example of the poet lowered to the level of a buffoon, where his image no longer retains what is essential. As far as the press was concerned, Valle-Inclán was nothing more than a picturesque individual. He himself was painfully aware of the vulgarity on the part of journalists who, having little affection for literature, invade the poet's world and use him as a source of trivial amusement. His famous testament, of which there are several versions, is addressed to the typical newshound who pursued and tormented him. In his biography, Gómez de la Serna sympathetically describes how this ordeal continued to the very end, with questions parodied from Valle-Inclán himself, such as "When do we give up the ghost, Don Ramón?" In his testament, the mood of which is comparable to that of Francois Villon, the poet condemned the kind of myopia which tarnished his own legend.

Yet that very legend—and I repeat—is the result of an imaginative capability which, though also the source of written works, should not be confined to them. It extends throughout the whole life of the man and pervades his every activity. Hence the unfortunate misinterpretations of which the paragraph by Maeztu quoted above is an excellent example. That he was mistaken in his approach, in my opinion, was due to the fact that the system of values governing Valle-Inclán's existence was an exceptional one in that it was built upon the primacy of the aesthetic. It is unusual, even among the most dedicated and sensitive artists, that aesthetics should prevail over all other values. We are safe in assuming that Garcilaso, a great lyric poet, visualized himself primarily as a soldier and a courtier; San Juan de la Cruz, as a man of the Church. Ortega y Gasset has submitted the plausible thesis that Velásquez considered himself essentially not a painter but a gentleman. Valle, on the other hand, saw both the world and himself as theatrical in its broadest sense. The Modernist school, whose tenets he shared, placed the aesthetic above all else. Such an emphasis, in the case of Valle-Inclán, is, I think, not so much the result of historical-cultural circumstances, as the display of his innermost being.

Of course, to point out his predilection for the aesthetic does not imply that an ethic is lacking, as some have been prone to believe. What happens is that, in him, ethics is modulated by aesthetics. Thus Valle-Inclán's life, so rich in colorful details and surrounded by legend, reveals an aspiration of dignity and greatness whose lofty moral qualities are undeniable. Gómez de la Serna recalls that, on different occasions Valle-Inclán, who was actually going hungry, would turn down friends who invited him to dinner, excusing himself with "I've just had something to eat" or "I have an appointment" (undoubtedly an appointment with hunger). These proud gestures, to be sure, have a beauty of their own. Even more important, however, is that underneath the outer form lay a stoic dignity whose essence is unquestionably moral. Furthermore, it is my belief that if the anecdotes concerning Valle-Inclán were carefully considered against this background, they would disclose a believable and, incidentally, a noble image of his personality; one very much in harmony with his written work. And this is because, as I have already suggested, his patterns of behavior tended to make an artistic creation out of his own life.

Once this point of view is accepted and his personality thus interpreted, most subjects of controversy surrounding Valle-Inclán will simply vanish. In this regard, let us consider for a moment the debate concerning his political affiliations or tendencies. The average man, and especially the newspaperman, thinks of politics as the basis of all other attitudes, when actually it should be seen as that aspect of morality which is applicable to the social order. And what was Valle-Inclán's stand regarding politics? It must be said that his fellow intellectuals of the same generation delighted in mystifying the public with their political statements. Unamuno's remarks were always aimed at shocking his readers and making them think after provoking indignation, and Azorin's often proved to downright scandalous. Valle-Inclán, at the beginning of his literary career, declared himself a Carlist. This was generally looked upon as a *boutade,* one of those quirks of Don Ramón which should not be taken seriously. And yet, in the face of the situation during the Spanish Restoration, into which he had been born and which all intellectuals agreed to be so negative, Valle-Inclán reacted by taking the Carlist position precisely because it was a lost cause, relegated to an irrevocable past. Where his early writings were concerned, this position led to his contributing to the Modernist aesthetic those colorful types who had disappeared forever (or so it was thought at the time) from the Spanish political scene and thus allowed themselves to be transformed ideally according to Romantic and Modernist fashions.

But when Valle-Inclán felt he had exhausted that aesthetic, another line of creation, even more inventive and more personal, began to unfold. The method of stylization earlier employed to acutely embellish certain realities of the past would be substituted by another which went in the opposite direction; that is, toward the grotesque and truculent, thus giving birth to what he called the *esperpento.* Clearly this type of deformation could most effectively be applied to immediate reality; it was the historical present, in some cases the very recent past, which lent itself to the systematic distortion which was the basis for Valle's new aesthetic. Now Don Ramón would expose the political situation against which the Carlists had so futilely rebelled, to the effects of his ridiculing technique.

At first glance it would seem that Valle's *political* position had not changed with the reversal of his aesthetic, but a closer look reveals that his new approach to the world led him to attitudes generally associated with the extreme left wing, even with anarchism. Does this mean, perhaps, that his *ideas* had changed? This is not exactly true. Basically they were the same; as always, they defied the usual classification. It would be foolish to try to attribute to Valle-Inclán a particular political ideology or loyalty to a given party or group. He lived according to standards of an eminently aesthetic nature, judging the world around him from a standpoint dictated by his unrelenting principles. This strength of character can be seen, all too clearly, in some of the anecdotes originated after the establishment of the last Spanish Republic and later collected by his biographers. His moral judgments, never formulated in the abstract but rather in response to his own extremely personal reactions, were also, and more importantly, aesthetic judgments.

This is the man, "feo, católico y sentimental" (as he described his character Bradomín) who, at the hour of his death, refused the last rites of the Church in a statement that he, as essentially a man of letters, had prepared for the occasion. It was not a time for jokes, the moment of truth had arrived. As we might have expected, this ultimate truth, for Valle-Inclán, would take on an artistic dignity befitting its profound significance.

To cast this aside as something marginal or accessory, and

simply limit our attention to his written works is to disregard the best means we have of understanding them. All art is the product of a creative spirit. In the case of Valle-Inclán, his written works were but one aspect of his overall artistic achievement.

ILDEFONSO MANUEL GIL

"INNOCENT VICTIMS" IN THE WORKS OF VALLE-INCLÁN

Translated by

DOUGLASS ROGERS

The illustrious teacher Amado Alonso, in his two excellent essays on Valle-Inclán, included today in the book *Materia y forma en poesía,* has left us the best guide for finding our way through the difficult and beautiful roads of Valle-Inclán's prose, a rich and complex prose, full of broad avenues, of secluded paths, of luxurious parks and mysterious labyrinths. And, more or less in passing (not in the text of the study itself but rather in a note), he divides Don Ramón's prose into two epochs.

What concerns us here is to take note of the venerable teacher's statement with respect to the position of the author in each one of these two epochs. He tells us that in the first "there is an attitude of scorn toward life, combined with an esthetic goal, that of the painter who throws back his head to observe every brush-stroke, in short, an attitude of withdrawal and contemplation from the artist's perspective."

In the second stage, the attitude is still basically the same but it is expressed in a different fashion:

> There is scorn, but of another type. That of the *Sonatas* was the authentic scorn of the person who disdains and removes himself; now it is one which joins contempt with reproach. The first Valle-Inclán remembers and develops; the second one lives and acts. The themes of the first Valle-Inclán, taken from the world literature, have a bookish tone, stylized in the extreme; those of the second one—themes of national life—reveal a stylized oral tone. (*op. cit.,* Gredos, Madrid, 1955; pp. 366–367).

This scornful attitude of the great writer whose memory is being so fittingly honored by this University is viewed by other critics as an attitude of indifference. Valle-Inclán would, accordingly, be the type of creator who lived removed from his creations, who thrust them into their destinies of joy and suffering, without ever revealing so much as a shadow of sympathy for them.

Although it is true that many examples could be put forth showing the scornful attitude, as well as many others demonstrating indifference, it is no less true that there are sufficient examples to indiciate a third position which is markedly different from these two attitudes.

A rereading of Valle-Inclán's complete works, undertaken with the aim of finding examples of this third point of view, has brought us to the conclusion that in his complex repertoire of characters may be found a category of individuals with a special destiny and a special treatment. The life, and even more, the death of those characters are the subject of the present study.

Valle-Inclán's statements on the point of view of the author toward his creations has been the subject of numerous quotes and various interpretations. His words have come to be accepted as a kind of esthetic dogma, without due credit being given to the fact that Valle-Inclán believed faithfully only in the concept of creative liberty for the artist, a belief which underwent no changes or limitations throughout his entire work.

In his excellent book *Las estéticas de Valle--Inclán,*[1] Díaz Plaja establishes a correspondence between the three *points of view* and the three *manners* of Valle-Inclán: a) Viewing the characters "from a kneeling position, as Homer saw his heroes," corresponds to the "mythical manner." b) Seeing them "eye-to-eye, as Shakespeare sees his," would be the perspective characteristic of the "ironical manner." c) Viewing them "beneath us, as did Cervantes, who constantly considered himself more sane than Don Quijote," would amount to the "degrading manner."

If the system of perspectives in these declarations appeared rather confusing, not in its conception but in its application to the literary work of Valle-Inclán, the confusion becomes complete in the correlation with *manners.* (Let us overlook the idea that the "eye-to-eye" view should produce only irony). Valle-Inclán viewed "from a kneeling position," or at least "from below," characters such as Adega and Don Juan Manuel de Montenegro, his two outstanding creations in the "mythical manner." And for all the others no possibilities remain other than the "ironical manner" or the "degrading" one.

Nevertheless, throughout the illustrious writer's entire work—not only its stages, or modes, or different styles, but throughout the amazing unity which underlies its rich variety of elements—a certain human condition may be found repeatedly, that of the "innocent victim," treated by the author with a most evident sympathy.

Let us begin by pointing out that we consider to be such a character one who, without being at all guilty, without any voluntary participation in the action, becomes a victim of the passions of others. He does nothing except suffer. And he is the victim of culpable acts, not of fortuitous events. Marginal characters, they are placed in the heart of the actions for the purpose of being harmed or destroyed. They are, thus, innocent victims of a cruelty which on occasions is exaggerated— to the extent of challenging reason or credibility.

Some of them survive, while others—the most significant ones —meet a violent death. This difference permits establishing two categories: the innocent victims who remain at the level of the drama and those who ascend to a tragic plane.[2]

The Dramatic Level

Examples of this type of innocent victim are Beatriz (from the story of the same name, in *Corte de Amor*, reproduced in *Jardín umbrío*), Eladia (from *Los cruzados de la causa* and *El resplandor de la hoguera*) Aunt Rosalba (from *Gerifaltes de antaño*) and the widow of a guard (from *La corte de los milagros*).

Beatriz is in the midst of that world of gloomy superstitions which so appealed to Don Ramón; the unfortunate girl has been the victim of the perversity of her confessor, a friar described as "a tall and dried-up old man, with an imperious and martial manner of walking." (Let us recall, in passing, that of the numerous clerics who appear in the pages of Valle-Inclán there are very few who do not receive a vilifying or demeaning treatment. Anticlericalism is a constant in the master's writings.)

In the view of those who live with Beatriz, in the manor house of the Countess of Porta-Dei, the girl is bewitched; the devil in her is fought by the priest with exorcisms and by the witch of Céltigos with black magic. Beatriz is contested for within the clutches of the devil. The Countess says of her daughter, "It terrifies me to hear her shout, to see her twist like a salamander in the fire . . ."; consequently, her appearance can scarcely surprise us: "The child, with eyes rolling and her dishevelled hair falling over her shoulders, lay writhing. Her blond, Magdalene-like head was banging against the wooden floor, and from her rigid and anguished brow flowed a thin stream of blood."

At the end of the story the witch's "condemnations" turn out to be as efficient a castigation for the guilt as the pious efforts of the priest were in discerning it. The body of the friar will appear floating on the waters of the river. Yet Beatriz's life has been forever ruined. The unfortunate girl has not been to blame; rather she is an innocent victim. "With terror and force they have taken advantage of her!" points out the priest after he, as her confessor, uncovers the secret of that hatred for holy things which Beatriz felt and which, needless to say, was not the mysterious consequences of some demonical force, but rather the understandable reaction of the young Countess to the conduct of her chaplain.

* * *

Eladia, the delicate little Galician girl, is a character enveloped in a halo of kindness which has its source in her own being; the author always presents her in this light of tenderness, radiating outward from within.

At the behest of Mother Isabel, the prioress of the convent of Viana del Prior, she has managed to get her sweetheart, the captain of a merchant ship, to face the storm in order to deliver a load of smuggled weapons to the Carlists. Bradomín, the sober gentleman "legitimist," directs the operation, assisted by priests and nuns and with the collaboration of don Juan Manuel Montenegro and his youngest son, "Cara de Plata."

The seaman wishes to weigh anchor without waiting for the loading of the goods; his duty is to save the ship and its crew. But Eladia is able to convince him to wait. The girl has committed these acts, but she has done so in complete innocence, under the weight of the irresistible pleadings of the nun and the "gentlemen". During the wait the ship sinks and the captain dies. Thus is Eladia's life dramatically modified; with the memory of her lost love, she becomes a novice in the convent. Mother Isabel feels herself to blame for the tragedy which has befallen Eladia, but the latter never directs a single reproach at her. She accepts her personal misfortune and later endeavors to help other unfortunates, accompanying Mother Isabel when the latter marches off to the battlefields to attend wounded Carlists.

Eladia is not a Carlist; she is simply a poor girl utilized by the political passions of others. And never for an instant is she presented without the sympathy of the author; her goodness, her resignation and sadness protect her from whatever connotation might not imply a sincerely compassionate vision.

The final chapter of *Los cruzados de la causa* is full of this kind of sympathy. In the dialogue between the nun and the novice the status of innocent victim of the latter is clearly brought out: Mother Isabel knows herself to be guilty; she feels like an executioner, and from this sentiment is born her expiatory decision to go to the battlefields to tend to the wounded. This trip is a central theme of *El resplandor de la hoguera* and a key to the understanding of the Carlist War Novels;[3] Eladia continues to be presented strictly from a point of view of respect and identification with her grief. The progress toward "esthetic deformation," toward the *esperpento*, so pronounced from the first to the second novels of the trilogy, will never touch Eladia. (Nor, on the other hand, will it affect Mother Isabel, about whom Valle-Inclán will write some of his most noble pages, those most impregnated with humanitarianism. The wounded which the nun had expected to care for were the Carlists; but once in the battlefield her initial intention becomes ennobled: the wounded which she sees turn out to be soldiers of the liberal army, and the distinctions between the sides are erased; the nun understands what her true duty is, for in pain all men are equal: " '¡Oh Lord, You are showing me that my hands would be cursed if they did not stanch the blood which is now being shed!' And all alone she marched down the muddy highway.")[4]

The final appearance of Eladia, in the last chapter of the novel we have been discussing, crystallizes her character in definitive fashion. When the grotesque Roquito came out from the fireplace which had been his hiding place, his eyes burning and his face looking like "a great black and red blister," "Eladia got up silently, and her soft hands, like a soothing balm, began to cure the wounded eyes of the sacristan, who knelt before her with his arms opened like a cross." And then the difference between Mother Isabel and Eladia is reiterated: the former feels herself guilty, while the latter is an innocent victim.

* * *

Aunt Rosalba is a strictly marginal character who on one occasion advances to the foreground, as the victim of the moral perversion or of the nefarious frivolity of Agila. This young aristocrat is a character worthy of attention, and in him Valle-Inclán presents a penetrating case of a "gratuitous crime"; but it is not he who interests us here, rather his victim.

Old Rosalba, the illegitimate sister of the Marquise of Redín, and as such, great aunt of Agila, forms part of the household on the hybrid level of family friend and trusted servant. Her witch-like appearance (as Emma Speratti Piñero has pointed out, Valle-Inclán's "mirrors" are involved here[5]) is belied by her kindness. Her words and deeds are full of dignity, even though she is only an insignificant little old lady. Perhaps it is the bleakness of her kindness and her destiny which constitute the remote, hidden causes of the agression:

> The old lady's devotion inspired in the soul of Agila an egoistic and cold spite. He would have desired that she take him straight to the side of his grandmother. Silently they started down the staircase. Agila looked at the old lady and felt tempted to push her and send her head over heels. It was a thought which showed in his eyes, the puerile and barbarous impulse of a cruel child. The long stairway was inviting, all of solid stone, rather dark, with the light of the doorway open to the huge foyer visible in the background. He stepped back a little and gave her a

> push. At the same time he felt a great coldness in his cheeks and a pressure in his heart. The old lady went rolling down with a deathly sound, and at her side the cruet bounced along with a hollow, metallic clucking.

Faced by her agressor, the stance adopted by Aunt Rosalba is precisely one of dissimulation, as a result of which the absurd depravation of the young aristocrat is more strikingly emphasized and denounced.

* * *

There is also an unnamed woman who appears as an example of a dramatic innocent victim. She is the widow of a guard whom some upstart young aristocrats have thrown out the window, in an impromptu encore to a typical spree. This poor fellow is a victim, of course, though not in the sense which concerns us here, being excluded because of his profession. Nevertheless, it may be observed that in these pages of *La corte de los milagros,* a novel at once historical and *esperpentesque,* replete with grotesque elements, the guard himself scarcely presents any degrading connotations. The esthetic degradation relates to the ethical degradation of the young aristocrats and their cohorts. For even though the unhappy man, shortly before being hurled through the window to the street, "smiled like a mask, through his great, shoe-black mustache," his attitude is that of one who is aware of being a victim, even if a shameful one, of an unjust society established to promote the interests of those in power.

The guard's widow is truly an innocent victim. It is significant that she is never actually present in the novel, except through references. That this miserable woman and her children should even exist is the most energetic condemnation of the senseless crime. There is no need for her to appear except as the widow, the woman whose suffering must be blamed on bad wine and on the wickedness of a few young dandies.

She is mentioned twice: first, when a way to hush up the

scandal is being sought, and gifts and bribes are being considered. The ridiculous Toñete advises, "The one who will have to be silenced with a few thousand is the dead man's widow," a grotesque statement which reflects only on the one who said it, without besmirching the disgraced wife. The situation is left perfectly clear when the author finished by saying, "Everyone understood that it was bound to cost a few *pesetas* to console that hoarse, unknown woman, who at that time was perhaps seated before the guard's body, in a distant neighborhood, moaning curses."

"Hoarse," "unknown," "perhaps," "distant neighborhood," are words which verify the accusing and sympathetic position of the author. The accusing spirit and sense of human solidarity are heightened when the mother of one of the brawlers and the sister of another personally try to succor the widow. Passing themselves off as members of the Society of St. Vincent de Paul, they go to visit the poor lady. The scene is unforgettable:

> "Does the widow of the guard live here . . .?"
> "The poor soul that a bunch of drunk fancy dans murdered last night? Yes, she lives here. And what of it? Are you by some chance asking after that poor woman?"
> The Marquise nodded an said, "We are from the Society of St. Vincent . . . and if she does live here we should like to see her."
> "She lives here all right! What do you expect the sorry creature to do, throw herself out of the window with her four children? Yes, she lives here, but she has gone out to look for work as a maid. She is a widow now and has to scrape by like the rest of us. I lost my husband in 'seventy-five, at the barricades of Antón Martín. That's where they sacrificed him for me."
> The Marquise touched the shoulder of her aged maidservant and discreetly passed her a few coins for her to give to the old lady.

> The latter looked at the coins with an ambiguous air, coveting them while at the same time scorning them: "Are they for me or for Macaria?"
> The Marquise, with a languid gesture muttered, "For you."
> The old lady seized her child by an ear. "Thank you, thank you. Thank the ladies, Celino. Wipe your nose and kiss their hands."
> Celino greeted them guffawing and grinning from ear to ear. The ladies climbed into their coach, and the Marquise stammered: "I think we were very lucky in not finding the poor woman in. It was a very risky business, Feliche. Fate might have had it that she would get suspicious and recognize us. We shall have Cayetana come and find out what this wretched family needs and help them out. But as for us, I think we should not return. I feel sick. It's terrible how these people live.!"

One may see in this case how, specifically through the words of the Marquise of Torre Mellada, the question is no longer limited to a confrontation with a victim of deeds executed by one or several persons, as previously, but rather refers to the injustice of a general social condition. The condemnation is extended to the group of brawlers and to a society as a whole, with no mirrors, concave or convex, turning the denunciation into caricature.[6]

* * *

In the same novel we find a most curious case of the presentation of a victim initiated in this same accusing tone—a veritable literature of denunciation—which is reversed later, when the character reappears, unnecessarily, bereft of all the dignity which he had acquired as the victim of a brutal injustice.

A hack bullfighter is found travelling without a ticket and is denounced by the conductor to the two *guardias civiles* serving on the train.

> Through two side windows of a third-class coach loomed the guns and three-cornered hats of the worthy team. Like a cat the adolescent shadow of a rogue slipped to the ground and then darted off through the fields. The train puffed. Then, from the same side of the car appeared the pair of gun barrels. They aimed. One shot, then another rang out and the fleeing rascal went headlong, feet on high in a convulsive dance.

Emphasizing this vicious abuse of power in an atmosphere of belligerence and brutishness ("the car was filled with belligerent, carnival-like shouting") with a technique of contrasts so characteristic of the Baroque and of Valle-Inclán, this passage shakes the reader into an unrestrained feeling of censure of brutality and injustice. The denunciation is reinforced by being carried to a symbolic level, with which the chapter closes: "The black silhouette of the train snaked along through the petrified sea of the plains of La Mancha. Trotting along behind, with lance poised in its socket, the picture of illusion under the full moon, the helmet, the shadow of Don Quijote; behind him he carried what looked like a straw dummy, legs and arms gone limp, exposing to the winds two holes in the lee of his ears."

But some pages further on, the bullfighter will reappear, limping from a bullet wound, his only reason for existing being to represent an unfortunate creature made fun of even by the poor country folk, who are not in the least friendly to the *Guardia Civil.* The tragic straw dummy has been changed into a grotesque dummy, a cranky cripple.

The Tragic Level

In the author's first book there is a character who comes to acquire the condition of victim in inexplicable fashion. It is Rosarito, from the story of the same name. But she is much different from the other cases which we have been examining. Both she and her destroyer are overly charged with *fin de siècle* estheticism. It is not a question of a gratuitous act, as in the case of the young Agila, but rather of a sadistic crime, in which death and eroticism are joined more harshly and nebulously than ever, even while allowing the persistent association of these two elements in all of Valle-Inclán's work.

Rosarito is the grandaughter of the Countess of Cela, with whom she lives in her Galician manor house. Listening to the chaplain of the house read the lives of saints, while doing delicate embroidery work, is what occupies the family soirées, which are presided over by the dozing grandmother. But the attention of the adolescent girl is occupied by a hazy and mysterious world of fantasy:

> Suddenly Rosarito raises her head and, as though in a daze, stares at the door to the garden, which opens out onto a mass of dark and mysterious foliage—and yet no more mysterious in reality than that white and pensive child. Seen by the soft light of the lamp, with her blond head in a divine foreshortening, the shadow of her eyelashes trembling on the marble-white cheek, her delicate and graceful bosom vaguely profiled over her fine waist and against the celestial blue damask of the settee, Rosarito brought to mind those innocent Madonnas painted against a background of stars.[7]

An ominous premonition of the girl's brings to the reader's attention the figure who is to be Rosarito's destroyer: none other than a certain Don Juan Manuel de Montenegro . . . a confirmed bachelor, a liberal conspirer, and an enemy of lineages and heraldry.[8]

Once this individual is present in the story, the crime comes about unexpectedly. There is only a cry in the silence of the night, then the discovery of the dead girl:

> Rosarito is lying there stiff, lifeless, white! Her cheeks are moistened by two tears. Her eyes have the fixed and terrifying stare of the dead. Across her slight body flows a stream of blood! . . . The gold pin, which only moments before still served to hold the child's hair, has been barbarously plunged into her breast, over her heart. Her golden hair flows over the pillow, tragically, magdalenically . . .

This "Modernist" heroine—like Beatriz and other female characters of the first works of Valle-Inclán—more than a living being, is a *motif*, a pretext for an esthetic game. His stories are narrated in a style very distant from that of the sentimental participation of the author; once the denunciation or accusation is discarded, not even an attitude of co-suffering is attained. The fact that the golden pin should be "Barbarously plunged" is not an indication which substantiates censure or protest on the part of the author. Perhaps we could apply here a statement of Bradomín's from *La corte de los milagros*: "Once again esthetics and acts of mercy have been at variance."

The first two innocent victims on a tragic level, who fulfill all the conditions for such, are two anonymous characters. The fact that they are unnamed is a quality which allows their individuality to be multiplied, elevated to its ultimate potential, thus making them representatives of an overly frequent human destiny.

The first of these, from *Los cruzados de la causa*, has found himself caught between two opposing forces, as if he symbolized the destiny of any country rent asunder by a civil war. He is a Galician boy who has been drafted by the liberal government and finds himself on guard duty in front of the convent of Viana del Prior while an inspection is carried out. The aristocrats of the city, the clergy and the nuns themselves deem the inspection a profanation; but in their church are hidden firearms which are to be sent to the Carlist army. The respect due the holy place has been lost by the rebels sooner than by the government forces; this point is clear, even though the sympathy of the author is with the conspirers.[9]

The women of the village react violently against the proceedings of the forces carrying out the inspection. Among them is the mother of the young sailor or *marinerito* (the diminutive form here emphasized the innocence of the victim, corresponding to his appearance: "He was small, happy, with childish eyes and cheeks browned by the sun and the wind") who, unjustly wrathfull about the involuntary participation of her son, pours cruel recriminations upon him. The pressure from his mother reaches such a degree that the boy throws down his gun and attempts to flee, an instinctive reaction to the situation in which he is caught between two antagonistic forces.

The persecution is presented with the full participation of the author; it is as though he were running alongside the boy, as if he too were about to receive the same bullets which will enter the young sailor's neck and leave him "sprawled on the sidewalk, face down, in a pool of blood."

The sailor's having been conscripted by pure force and the fact that there really were arms hidden in the convent are points which stress the quality of innocent victim; the occasional sympathy of the author for the Carlist cause has not prevented the death, here in the pages of the book, from attaining the pathetic value of a condemnatory outcry from which none of the factions which voluntarily participate in the war is excused. The possible intention of the author to have the blame fall only on one side was superseded in the writing of these pages.

The other unnamed victim, in *El resplandor de la hoguera,* is a child, the son of a baggage man in the liberal army. In the midst of a fray his donkey escapes, and the boy runs after it:

> The animal, freed of the weight of its rider, shook and stretched its back and brayed so sonorously that the

> thousand-year-old echo of those mountains might be awakened, recalling the sound of the horn of Roland.[10] After catching the animal, the boy rode along happily, and spurring him on with his heels, trotted into the midst of the infantrymen. Near the bridge, a bullet opened a hole in his forehead. He remained atop his mount, his hands yellow and one eye hanging over a cheek, suspended by a bloody strip of flesh. Slowly he began to lean over and finally fall, whereupon the donkey stood motionless beside him.

Later, the father will try to rescue the body, but he will have to relinquish it under the boots of the soldiers coming and going in combat, with which the pathos of the situation is intentionally reinforced by the author. Although an effort is then made to end the chapter on a spirited note, the fact that the Carlist volunteers, "upon seeing the forward push of the troops, stood their ground, firing and exulting with joyous voices, as farmers in harvest of Basques dancing the *zorcico,*" cannot undo the impression created by the death of the child. In this final sentence of Chapter XIX of *El resplandor de la hoguera* there is much more rhetoric than conviction.

* * *

Although the youngest daughter of Princess Gaetani, in the *Sonata de primavera,* dies as the result of an accident, thus excluding her as a representative of the character-type we are studying, there is a small child who dies violently as a consequence of cruelty, superstition and base passions. He is, in a sense, the central character of *El embrujado*, about whom revolve the culpable activities of the adults, ranging from avarice and fraud to crime; the child dies of a bullet wound, and it is not significant that it was not fired at him but at the person carrying him. In the accusations hurled by certain characters against others, their own blame is placed in relief, as is also that which surpasses the individuals and is associated with a society sustained by injustice.

Cruelty and greed show up anew in connection with another luckless individual: the "idiot child" of Juana la Reina in *Divinas palabras*. But this helpless cripple receives a different treatment and is, in his deformity, simply the object of esthetic manipulations. Wrong is shown through the simple exposition of the facts, but nothing supports any claim to an ethical position on the part of the author. Through his monstrosity the character comes to invalidate the condition of victim at least in the sense being dealt with here.

The same thing occurs with the crazy daughter of Santos Banderas, brought to the attention of the author by the daughter of Aguirre el Traidor, the curious historical personage so evident in the genesis of *Tirano Banderas*.

* * *

In the eleventh scene of *Luces de Bohemia* another anonymous innocent victim is presented: "A bewildered group of neighborhood women, on the sidewalk. A woman, breast bared and voice hoarse, holds in her arms her dead child, its brow pierced with a bullet hole."

We will learn that this bullet has been fired by the police in putting down a workers' demonstration. The mother's lamentations are punctuated with insults hurled at the police. And Max Estrella, filled with respect, asks, "Who is that crying? Whose shouts of outrage are those?," and later confesses, "That tragic voice has shaken me!" and again, "That voice has pierced me . . . Never have I heard a voice expressing such tragic anger!"

Since to that impression is added that of the killing of the Catalonian worker who had been a cellmate of Max's in jail, it is not surprising that the delirious poet should feel at once rage and shame. His words leave no room for doubt:

> I can no longer shout . . . I'm dying of rage! . . . I am chewing thistles . . . The Black Legend, in these malingering days, is the history of Spain. Our life is a Dantesque circle. Rage and shame!

Even though the scene ends with a few grotesque words from the puppet-like Don Latino de Hispalis, the condemnation of the police brutality is done simply by presenting the dead child and the mother, hoarse from crying and shouting.

It should be noted that the scene is an interruption in the development of the action; the tenth scene would otherwise be linked perfectly with the twelfth, with no let-up whatsoever in the dramatic development. The episode has been put in by the author as accusatory testimony against official violence, against brutality and injustice.

The element of chance has not been utilized capriciously, for in such police operations the death of someone wholly unrelated to the circumstances is not an unusual occurrence. And a capricious use of chance might have invalidated, or at least weakened, the value of the testimony. This is why, for the purposes of our study, the daughter of the cuckold, Don Friolera, does not attain the category of innocent victim—even though she may be a victim and a blameless one. Hers is a death which is necessary to the sense of the work, inseparable from it; therefore, it is an element of literary technique and not a matter of moral values . . . which are what we are dealing with in this study.

Another child, the son of Zacarías el Cruzado, attains a position in the absolute foreground in the recounting of innocent victims. Since *Tirano Banderas* is the best *esperpento* novel, this victim acquires the highest significance. In a novelistic world so completely shaped by "systematic deformation," this character alone stands free of such an implacable atmosphere. His presence even comes to effect a change in style: the prose sheds its Baroque luxuries and takes on a special, austere sobriety, with expressive touches which become truly poignant. The deforming vision, which is applied without fail to all the other characters, is very cautiously avoided here. In the mother there are still some overly picturesque touches, although I believe that she also received some of the special treatment, as if the son projected over her a light to save her from the usual connotations of *the esperpento.* In the conception of the child there is nothing more than the innocent creature overpowered by injustice and by cruelty. The episode (Fourth Part, Fourth Book, IV) is extremely short. The tyrant's police have come to detain Zacarías, and when they don't find him they arrest his wife. Since "the police station is no foundling asylum," the officers leave the child abandoned:

> The infant, in the slimy pool, was crying, surrounded by the grunting pigs. The mother, while being shoved by the gendarmes, turned her head and with heart-rending cries said: "Come! Don't be afraid! Come! Run!"
>
> The child ran for a moment, then stopped in the middle of the road, calling to the mother. One officer turned around and frightened the child, who stopped short, crying and slapping his own face. Hoarsely the mother shouted: "Come! Run!"
>
> But the child did not move. He stood sobbing at the edge of the pond, watching the distance grow between him and his mother.

Here is a point of view which was not included in the author's famous statements. He is not viewing from above, nor from below, nor even on a level. All of these are exterior perspective, whereas here the vision is not from the outside the character but from inside of him. In the denouement of this episode, Valle-Inclán viewed from the standpoint of the grief of the child, while sharing it with him.

Later, when the pigs devour the child and there is nothing more left of him than an incriminating "bloody shred," the theme provides several macabre, cruel scenes. But as long as the child is alive and suffers he is treated with the greatest expressive sobriety and with the greatest sympathetic respect. This is a treatment which the author reserved for very few of his characters, for very few who, in one fashion or another, do not happen to be victims of something or someone.[11]

Elsewhere I had occasion to note how the author shared in the grief of some of his characters; in that instance I referred only to *Luces de Bohemia.*[12] There, the daughter of the great bohemian Max Estrella is to a large extent, an innocent victim. In her and in the characters just pointed out, who stem—some more, some less—from this condition, we have seen not only the co-suffering of the author, linked to each individual case in different degrees and variants, but also a reiterated attitude of protest against the baseness and brutality of some individuals and against the blameworthy indifference of the others.

This is a view which, by being reiterated and intensified extends to society as a whole and even to the very absurdity of life.

NOTES

[1] Ed. Gredos, Madrid, 1965. Concerning the statements by Valle and his relation to the three styles, see pp. 134, 175 and 176.

[2] Of course the terms "dramatic" and "tragic" are used only as regards the final destiny of the character, devoid of any other implications.

[3] In a forthcoming essay, "Frustración de la epopeya: la trilogía de *La Guerra Carlista*," I study this aspect of Valle-Inclán's work.

[4] Mother Isabel is one of the characters most "respected" by the author. This nun, the sister of Concha (*Sonata de Otoño*), must not be confused with the other Isabel—so different!—from the same volume of the Memoirs of Bradomín.

[5] See "El Esperpento" in *La elaboración artística en Tirano Banderas*, México, 1957, pp. 86 ff.

[6] In the final version of *La corte de los milagros,* which the newspaper *El Sol* published in pamphlet form, this passage appears considerably altered. I wish only to point this out now, as I intend to comment on the variants elsewhere.

[7] The story "Rosarito" went from *Femeninas* to other books; it is now included in all the editions of *Jardín umbrío.*

[8] This "false appearance" of the hero of the *Comedias Bárbaras*, which the author will resolve later with a simple name change is very pertinent to the question of the genesis of the famous character; we shall soon publish a study entitled "Indeciso origen de Bradomín y don Juan Manuel de Montenegro," in which an explanation of this confusion is undertaken.

[9] See note 3.

[10] Observe the *esperpentesque* tone of this paragraph, not at all infrequent in the trilogy of *La Guerra Carlista.*

[11] I would acknowledge that it is very much in evidence in the anarquist of *Luces de Bohemia*; this character is a victim of injustice, but he is not to be included for obvious reasons in the category of innocent victims: he has participated voluntarily; he is a fighter. In *Tirano Banderas* occasional scenes can be found in which the jailed liberals are presented with a certain respect (for example, the last paragraph of Chap. V of the First Book, Part Five), although at other times they appear as caricatured as their enemies.

[12] "From Baroja to Valle-Inclán," *Cuandernos hispanoamericanos*, No. 178, October, 1964.

JOSÉ RUBIA BARCIA

THE ESPERPENTO: A NEW NOVELISTIC DIMENSION

Testamento

Te dejo mi cadaver. Reportero
El día que me lleven a enterrar
Fumarás a mi costa un buen veguero,
Te darás en la Rumba un buen yantar.

Y luego de cenar con mi fiambre
Adobado en tu prosa gacetil,
Humeando el puro, satisfecha el hambre,
Me injuriará tu dicharacho vil.

Te dejo mi cadaver. Verme ingrato
Harto de mi carroña, ingenuamente
Dirás gustando del bicarbonato:
Que Don Miguel no muera de repente.

In the spring of 1893, Valle-Inclán was twenty-six years old and had arrived at the provincial capital of Pontevedra, where he had decided to settle down, at least for a while. He had just come back from Mexico and even his closest friends had difficulty recognizing him. When they had last seen him before his Mexican trip, there was nothing in his outward appearance to distinguish him from many another young man of the middle or upper-middle class: elegantly dressed, meticulously clean, his face shaven daily, wearing a well-kept, long-pointed mustache, rimless pince-nez glasses attached to his lapel with a black ribbon, and on top of his head the inevitable derby hat.[1] But now, he looked completely different; the change had been dramatic. The formerly sought-after elegance had given way to a "*rara catadura*," made up of a long beard, a luxuriant head of hair, a long cassock-like robe, a wide *chambergo* (broad-brimmed soft hat), and on his nose huge tortoise-shell-rimmed glasses. All in black: hair, cassock, trousers, boots, and even the rims of the glasses were almost black. "In the peaceful streets of Pontevedra," says a witness, "his presence had the impact of an extraordinary event. [At first] his peculiar appearance baffled the cunning gossipers and defied the jokes of the idle spectators."[2] But not for long. The same witness informs us that although he himself, at the time only a child, felt respect and amazement whenever he saw "that small but wild and arrogant figure"[3] going by, others ended up by reacting in a much different way. Galicians are well known for their sense of humor and for their some times corrosive irony. Valle-Inclán, himself a Galician, was later on to prove his mastery of these supposedly racial traits, but at the moment he was one of its victims. During the three years of his stay in Pontevedra, he was laughed at many times and was made the butt of innumerable practical jokes. It is even said that he finally left for Madrid because he could no longer stand the frequent calls of barbers sent to his home by the pranksters.[4] It is more than probable that the word he heard most those days, to define the impression he gave others, was the word *esperpento,* a popular synonym of "scarecrow."[5]

Valle-Inclán's "disguise" was undoubtedly a first and definite step toward building up an *image* that he needed to project. The next step was to try it out and to begin acting on a bigger and more adequate stage. He therefore moved to Madrid for the second time in his life. Ricardo Baroja, a brother of Pío the novelist, gives us his impression of Valle-Inclán the first time he saw him around 1897, in a *café madrileño*:

> . . . there sat a dark young man, with a long beard and a great mane, thin as a mummy. He was dressed in black; he had on his head a grayish plush *chambergo*, with a tall cone-shaped crown and wide brim. The corners of his high, starched shirt collar stuck out threateningly on both

> sides of his extremely black beard, which was trimmed in the fashion of the Ninevites of the XIXth century BC. Beneath the beard one could just barely make out the dangling ends of a wide black silk cravat. The cravat so dear to romantic spirits!
>
> I did not dare look directly at him. The strange character responded to the curious glances of those in the café with a brazen and insulting air and flashed the gleam of the dark-rimmed glasses astride his long nose at anyone who stared at him a bit insistently.[6]

Ramón Gómez de la Serna, recalls the Valle-Inclán of about the same time as "the best masquerade figure walking down the Calle de Alcalá," and adds:

> I remember having seen him going by, stiff and proud, yet ducking now and then behind the portable bullfight poster racks, which he used like bullring refuges against the verbal goring of those yelling "long-haired poet" at him.[7]

Valle-Inclán, all through his life, would try to attract public attention, in a kind of defiant manner, at first with his strange "outward" appearance and, later on, by means of peculiar actions, clever anecdotes, mordacious answers, and a constant display of wit. Little by little he was to become a legend in his own time, or—to use Salaverría's definition—a "*divo*."[8]

In direct relation with Valle-Inclán's effort to build up a public image, was the opposite tendency to carefully hide his intimate nature or inner self. Manuel Azaña tells us, in one of the most illuminating essays ever written on Valle-Inclán the man, that one day he came upon him asleep in a café, and the first thing he said upon waking up and seeing all the eyewitnesses was; "Yes, indeed! Poets have to be absurd men!"[9] Azaña says that the character Valle-Inclán made of himself in daily life, was that of "a demigod motivated by a desire for absolute justice," and continues:

> His hates, his verbal cruelty, his intransigence, can offer the justification that they originate from acceptable motives of public interest. He is a hero devoid of compassion, who has thrown many stones, because he was without sin. Understandably enough, he takes his stand on the extreme opposition side. He pillories mediocrity and evil; he is a foretaste of the Last Judgement for the vulgar, the hypocrites, the opportunists; he is a shy person shouting his aversions. But the justice he so deeply loves has not been learned from others nor has it been derived from any legal code. Valle-Inclán is the man with his own law, who scorns the social and legal hierarchy because *it is rotten.*[10]

Ramiro de Maeztu insisted that there was a separation, a clear dichotomy, between the inner man Valle-Inclán, on the one hand, and Valle-Inclán's work and his influence on others, on the other. Maeztu's preference is clearly for the exterior image or public character, of whom he said: "It is certain that nothing like Valle-Inclán has been seen in modern times even in Paris, Berlin, London or New York."[11]

Nevertheless, it would be a mistake to think that the exterior image projected by Valle-Inclan was merely the result of spontaneous conduct, rather than a conscious effort to build up, and follow through, an exemplary life without paying due tribute to the worldly temptations and weaknesses of ordinary human beings.[12] In a saint-like manner, but without the consolation of a firm religious faith, Valle-Inclán went through life suffering all kinds of privations, and refusing to share in the benefits of human society if these did not agree with the rigid demands of his conscience. Dr. Domingo García-Sabell, a close friend of Valle-Inclán in the last year of his life, a writer and critic, and also a trained psychiatrist, asks: "What was there behind his invectives, behind his clamorous indignation?" And he answers: "It was, without a doubt, a very tight and strict system of moral and cultural values." And further:

> ... he gave the impression of being [at times] an extreme denier, an anachronic anarchist and, in truth, he was only an *outsider*, a displaced person, a marginal man; one of those men who are, and at the same time are not, in the world around them, who *understand* and do not *take part*. And because they understand, they *judge*. And because they judge, they *condemn*.[13]

Up to the very last minutes of his life, Valle-Inclán took care to maintain the "inner logic" of the amazing character he had become. It is also Dr. García-Sabell who tells us the following moving and very revealing anecdote:

> ... When Valle-Inclán was already at the point of death, I received a hurriedly pencilled note, in which Don Ramón said: "Please come. The horrible pain is back again and *I am afraid that I will begin complaining like a woman!*" Now the circumstances were real, ferociously real—a tumor was eating away his insides—and his virile, fearful reaction allowed a glimpse of the stoic temper which the great writer had wrought and to which at the same time he did homage. Now Don Ramón was touching bottom, with his two feet on reality and, nevertheless, he was still obediently following the imperatives of certain ideal, schematic, and literary mandates.[14]

When Valle-Inclán died on Sunday, January 5, 1936, he left behind, on the one hand, enough material for a "Cervantine novel"[15] of his own life, and, on the other, a considerable amount of written words, structured over the years in more or less artistic units. These he had conceived, perfected and sometimes laboriously worked over in a long process, which reached its highest point with the discovery of what he decided to call *esperpentos*,[16] late in the second decade of the XXth century.

To find out what the meaning, the importance and the rightful place of the *esperpentos* is in the general panorama of creative writing, it will be necessary to go back in time.

* * * * *

The end of the XIXth century saw the end also, in most European countries, of the cultural premises that had made possible, since the Renaissance, the appearance and continuous cultivation of what was commonly to be known as the "modern novel." Its prototype was *Don Quijote,* the perfect incarnation of the literary hero. Ever since its beginning with Cervantes, the most basic and recurrent trait of the novel has been the acceptance of a functional discrepancy between what one is "underneath" and what one becomes in life for others.[17] This is expressed in Spanish by means of the verbs *ser* and *parecer,* with all sorts of variations: from an uncommon "parecer" to a common "ser"; from an uncommon "ser" to a common "parecer"; from an uncommon "ser" and "parecer" to the non-"ser", and so on, but always with a horizon of values acting as a live magnet for the positive hero, or as a dead magnet for the negative hero, or by another name, the anti-hero. The literary world reflected, in a symbolical and condensed way, the intrinsic duality of human nature, which is also present in the duality of human consciousness.[18] But something happened to the novel after Galdós, Pereda and Pardo Bazán in Spain; Balzac, Flaubert and Zola in France; Dickens, Thackeray and Meredith in England; Dostoyevsky and Tolstoy in Russia; and other major XIXth century novelists in other countries. No longer was the basic novelistic tenet of the duality of human life felt to be justified on philosophical or even imaginative grounds and, hence, to be able to support or enrich the spiritual and esthetic experience of the reader. New conceptions of reality and of personality began to operate in the subconscious mind of the artist and, as a consequence, every device previously used for the creation of the novel and every aspect of novelistic reality was now questioned: space, and objects in space, as parallel reflections of something existing in the *real* world; chronological or clock time as the locale of action; logical plots developed as sequences of cause and effect; the creation of believable characters in the process—through action and motivation—of becoming or disintegrating; the use of dialectic or Socratic dialogue to underline the separateness of human entities; and many others. Emphasis on logical interrelation between the physical and the spiritual, the outside and the inside, the *parecer* and the *ser,* existence and being, was going to be replaced by emphasis on man's inner, mental and emotional life, without any assurance of the independent projection of any "objects." The predominant attitude of the writer was now going to be what the phenomenologists call *epoché*,[19] or abstention, in regard to an object or a proposition, whose existence is considered to be predetermined and conditioned by intentionality and essence (not appearance).

Edmund Husserl was perhaps the first to say that the world *is there* before *it is* anything, but that only human consciousness gives it significance and reality, and inversely that consciousness cannot be conceived without the world. Both world and consciousness exist, therefore, in a sort of fluid and mutually illuminating relation, but never the one without the other. The natural deduction from phenomenological theory is the denial of the traditional, idealistic and rationalistic concept of the inner man as an abstract and immutable entity or, what would amount to the same thing, the affirmation of the impossibility of the existence of an integral and crystallized, or fixed, personality capable of moving outside itself, in an also "fixed" or independent outside reality.

Max Scheler and Nicolai Hartmann went a step further when they considered all values as "objects" in the phenomenological sense. As a result, modern axiology has been predicating that the conception of the world, the meaning of culture, and even man himself are directly related to, and dependent on, the realization of personal or collective values. José Ortega y Gasset, through his periodicals *España* (1914) first, and *Revista de Occidente*

(1923–1936) afterwards, plus his own publishing house and his own original books, was in the Spanish-speaking world the main exponent and popularizer of the new philosophical tendencies, of which he also became an important pillar and to which he made outstanding contributions. Post-Kantian non-positivistic thinking seems to fascinate the Spaniards (not only Ortega, but also Unamuno, García Morente, Gaos, Zubiri, etc.) as if, for the first time, a link between deep national spiritual currents and predominant European thought could be established. That would explain the fact that the key works of such representative German philosophers as Wilhelm Dilthey or Martin Heidegger were commented upon and translated into Spanish long before they became generally known in English or even in French. The same phenomenon occurs, even earlier, with Unamuno's interest in the Danish Kierkegaard, the recognized fountainhead of Existentialism, who will not be assimilated into the mainstream of Western thought until years later. There was something in Spanish traditional culture strangely akin to the tendencies now becoming dominant, as if the modern world and modern man were beginning to look at themselves with Spanish eyes. No other explanations can be found for the sudden bursting upon the international scene of such Spanish names as Gaudí, Picasso, Miró, and Dalí, in the spatial arts; and the appearance in Spain of the philosophical schools of Madrid and Barcelona, the so-called Generation of 1898, and the two succeeding literary generations.

At this point, it will not be amiss to underline the universality of the changes that were taking place. But we must allow for one difference in relation to Spain and the novel. No other country in Europe had contributed so much to the origin, birth and variety of the novel as Spain, beginning with *La Celestina* and continuing with the sentimental, Moorish, pastoral, picaresque and exemplary novels, to end up with the universal Cervantine or modern novel. It might even be possible to look upon Santa Teresa's *Vida* as the first seed of the future "stream-of-consciousness" novel. It was, therefore, only natural to expect that Spain would also be the first country, and the one most free to experiment in our time with new novelistic *formulae,* without falling back on what had already been tried in its own past.[20] For modern Spanish authors, it was enough to keep an ear close to the ground to be able to hear the demands of the time and to respond in kind with a wide range of experimentation, which sprang up as the normal growth of an appropriate soil. The main products of that experimentation, among which there is no apparent connection, are: the "pseudo-action" novel of Baroja, the "nivola" of Unamuno, the "atemporal narration" of Azorín, the *esperpento* of Valle-Inclán, the "poematic" creations of Ayala and Miró, and the "disjointed" utterances of Gómez de la Serna. On the other hand, what Sartre in France has called the *anti-roman,* and what after *The Erasers* (1953) by Alain Robbe-Grillet has been named the *nouveau roman,* comes much later and follows one single direction. It is the product of cerebration rather than of spontaneity, of reflection rather than of intuition, as if destined to prove an *a priori* conception of what ought to be, and subordinate esthetic joy to the enjoyment of knowledge, an almost permanent trait of French culture. Alain Robbe-Grillet, Michel Butor, Natalie Sarraute and Claude Simon, to name only the most outstanding representatives of the latest movements, all have in common a lesson which was learned, though this has not always been confessed, from a rich variety of predecessors, among whom the Spanish Unamuno (previously digested by Sartre and Camus) occupies a very important place. There is no denying that the *nouveau roman* school, carried prior experimentation and insights through to their last consequences, making good use not only of Unamuno's "nivola," but also of all the innovations brought about by other cultivators of an untraditional novel, like their own Proust—and, naturally, Sartre and Camus—, besides such other foreigners as Franz Kafka, James Joyce, Dorothy Richardson, Virginia Woolf, William Faulkner, all of them more or less read and recognized in the period between the two great World Wars, or even later, and of course long after some of the above-mentioned Spaniards.

Another reason to perhaps explain the priority of Spanish experimentation with the novel might be that Spain had touched bottom before any other great European country. What for Europe and the world at large was the meaning and the impact of the First World War, had its counterpart, in several common aspects for Spain, in the realization during the last decade of the XIXth century that old ideals and concepts—political and otherwise—were no longer valid. The loss to the United States, after the Spanish-American War, of the last remnants of the old empire, brought home dramatically the fact that something had ended definitely and something new would have to begin. A look to the rest of Europe did not give rise to much hope. The cracks in the old national structures were too apparent and, all over, a type of human individual who gave allegiance to humanity instead of the nation of his birth began to appear. The use that the most powerful European nations had been making of applied scientific knowledge had given a *coup de grâce* to the popular optimism of the West with its XIXth-century dream of indefinite progress, not only materially but also morally and spiritually. In its place, a feeling of a crisis in traditional values was permeating everything.

* * *

The role of Valle-Inclán as an important innovator, among his novelistic peers, developed slowly and did not reach its climax until the second decade of the XXth century. But he acquired very early a consciousness of the cultural and social circumstances in which he felt himself submerged. In the preface to a book by a friend, he reminisces about their youthful years at the end of the XIXth century when both arrived in Madrid. From this preface come the following thoughts:

> Grotesque Spanish times [were those] with everything sounding like counterfeit coins! All values had become debased: History, Politics, the Military, the Academies. Never had what by then began to be known as the Great Press—G.P.—, been so mercenary. The anagram (*sic*) conveys a wicked suggestion!
>
> . . . .
>
> Alienated from Spanish life, without a single bond through which to be benefitted by it, we [both] have contemplated with a good-humored look thirty years of history.[21]

But the reminiscences end, and Valle-Inclán comes back to the present, to the time he is writing the preface, probably coincidentally with the *coup d'état* of General Primo de Rivera (September, 1923):

> With these merry recollections I do not mean to imply that times have changed. Plumes and sashes are flashier than ever, and so are the speeches and toasts to celebrate glorious military retreats. Consistency is a Spanish virtue, and if the farce seems to have been changed around, it is because the number of fools has increased.[22]

Valle-Inclán's own consistency, in thought and conduct, is illustrated in this other paragraph, written early in 1902:

> And inside this obstinate rose that is my soul, I laugh at everything divine and at everything human, and believe only in beauty.[23]

And in a sort of chaotic enumeration of ingredients, he adds:

> I do not smoke, I do not drink, I hate *cafés* and bullfighting, religion and militarism, the accordion and capital punishment.[24]

There is no doubt that in the particular case of Valle-Inclán, the unexpected and unpopular dictatorship of Primo de Rivera exacerbated his dissatisfaction with the "establishment"—national and international—, but it is also clear that the tendency to be dissatisfied had old and deep roots and was not a typically and exclusively Spanish phenomenon. Let us look, for instance, at what the Italian novelist, Alberto Moravia, has to say about the years immediately after the First World War, and this could probably be taken as an expression of concensus among European writers of that time:

> . . . The fact is that I started to write in 1925 . . . and at that time there were very few or no values at all which, after the terrible crisis of the so-called twenties, resisted a close examination. Everything in this faraway time seemed tottering, inconsistent, contradictory, and false. There were only a few things which seemed to me solid and true and those things were connected with nature and with the less objectionable and analysable and ineffable sides of the human soul.[25]

Coming back to Valle-Inclán, he looked upon Cuban independence and the Mexican and Russian revolutions with great sympathy, and was conscious that, the latter especially, was the result of the great changes dramatized and brought to the surface by the First World War. He would have liked some of these changes to have taken place in his own Spain. But, instead, what did take place in Spain was that the Socialist-oriented general strike of 1917 ended in failure; that the Moroccan colonial war went from bad to worse with the shameful disaster of Annual (1921); and that, to end all and maintain the *status quo*, the King, the Church, the politicians and the Armed Forces dug up the almost forgotten XIXth century tradition of the "pronunciamiento," to the dismay of the progressive forces of the political spectrum who had been under the impression that those days were gone forever.

The recently established dictatorship made Valle-Inclán feel that he could not go on cultivating an exquisite art, with apparent disregard for everyday life and problems. To the question: *What are we writers supposed to do?* Valle-Inclán had already answered in 1920: "Not art. We must not cultivate Art now, because it is immoral and miserable to go on playing in these times. The first thing is to bring about social justice."[26]

However, one thing is the conscious purpose of the artist and quite another is its realization and the goals attained. Valle-Inclán, now in his fifties, could not cease to be what he already was, as a writer and as a human being as well. It is on what he really was that he could continue building his artistic world. As can be guessed, his definitive "image" was by this time formed and established, as was the main body of preferences, constant traits, and formal bases for his creative approach. At this point, the main difference from what was going to follow, seemed to be his decision to bring image and art together to bear upon the surrounding society. All previous experiences and efforts, seen retrospectively, looked like the right preparation for the birth of a new artistic structure. The grown-up human *esperpento* was at last ready to produce literary *esperpentos.* That he succeeded was not definitely proved until 1927, when *La hija del capitán* ('The Captain's Daughter') reached the streets. The reaction of the dictatorial government was violent and at the same time extremely eloquent. The Madrid newspapers were ordered to publish the following note:

> General Security Headquarters, carrying out government orders, has directed the withdrawal from circulation of a booklet, entitled *La hija del capitán,* which the author himself defines as an *esperpento:* since it does not contain a single line that does not offend good taste and does not fail to revile highly respectable social classes by means of the most absurd of plots. If any part of such booklet could be published, it would be clear that the government's decision is not inspired in an intolerable and narrow judg-

> ment but exclusively in that of preventing the circulation of those works that can only result in the prostitution of taste through an assault on good customs.[27]

Valle-Inclán's written words and his way of expressing himself in everyday life had at last coincided and become one. The mask which for a long time had been worn by the man and the author, upon falling away revealed that in his case the mask and the real face had become identical. Perhaps the motivating force had been a strong personal moral reaction, preceded by the realization that the clearest symptom of the time he was living in was the double identity of "mask" and "face" in the living individual who represented old hierarchies and ideals. Valle-Inclán must have felt that his intuitions were confirmed when he saw Luigi Chiarelli's play *La maschera e il volto* staged in Madrid at the end of 1923 by the Italian theatrical company of Dario Niccodemi.[28] He could not pretend any more and was ready to pay any price for an absolute sincerity. As is well known, from April 10 to April 25, 1929, he was incarcerated in a Madrid jail by the government. The note given to the press—and its peculiar style provides grounds for believing it was probably written by the dictator himself—read:

> The distinguished writer and eccentric citizen, Sr. Valle-Inclán, is also responsible for the order for his arrest, because on refusing to pay the two-hundred-fifty *pesetas* fine that had been imposed on him for an infraction against the government, with the intent of sparing him the loss of his freedom, he uttered such insults against the authorities and such destructive attacks against the established social order, that it has become impossible to exempt him from punishment as intended . . .[29]

This public characterization of the person and of his work, at this particular moment, and probably by the highest representative of the "establishment," gives us valuable clues which it will be worthwhile to follow through. In summary, Valle-Inclán is now recognized as a "distinguished" writer, a bad citizen, an independent or alienated character, an antagonizer of the established social order; and the author of late works called *esperpentos*, with "absurd plots" that provoke violent reactions on the part of the hierarchy of the country, which feels insulted by the author's opinions. On the other hand, nobody doubts his personal integrity, which gives him all the moral and intellectual authority needed to become not a humorous but a satirical writer. This distinction is important because humor tends indirectly toward the reinforcement of individual and collective values,[30] whereas satire has the opposite effect because of its exploitation of differences in judgments of value, especially among groups. That is why tyrants are always willing to allow a certain type of jokes, but will never stand for real satire embodied in a work of art by a "distinguished" creator. Modern axiology predicates that the work of art is the ideal fictitious place for the interplay of all kinds of values, and that even the esthetic value of the work of art itself is the product of that interplay in contact with, and against, the unchangeable physical-casual world, which appears as valueless. Art is the most worthwhile human activity and its axiological aspects "show that it is more than a game that goes with life. *Art* is an actual part of life, it is its *ideal axiological aspect*."[31] If we accept this, the satirical author will have to be above values, as will the independent or alienated character (the bad citizen, for the authorities) that Valle-Inclán was.

But there is still more. The function of efficiently antagonizing the "established social order" would require draining oneself of immediacy, of pressing needs, of identification with country and countrymen, because "*if satire seeks to degrade the collective values of a certain group or the individual values of a certain person, it is to bring about the final triumph of the universal values of humanity*, which have been supplanted or obfuscated by collective or individual values. In short, satire is therefore capable of uniting humans on a higher plane, the plane of universal values" . . .[32] Many texts of Valle-Inclán can be quoted to show clearly that this goal and its preconditions had found gradual expression in his life, in his work and in his esthetic consciousness, making of him, after the discovery of the "*esperpentos*", the first Spanish satirist with a universal message, a message to which even personal life was completely subordinated after having been conditioned for total agreement. From lectures he gave, the following thoughts are culled:

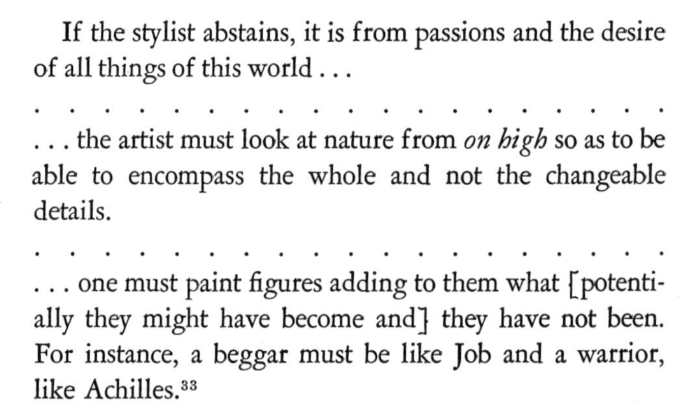

> If the stylist abstains, it is from passions and the desire of all things of this world . . .
>
> . . . .
>
> . . . the artist must look at nature from *on high* so as to be able to encompass the whole and not the changeable details.
>
> . . . .
>
> . . . one must paint figures adding to them what [potentially they might have become and] they have not been. For instance, a beggar must be like Job and a warrior, like Achilles.[33]

The last thought can be interpreted as implying the total dehumanization of characters, the intention to carry them to a unidimensional extreme, to the annulment of all traces of "inner duality." What is involved here is a decision on the part of the author to reduce his characters to their essence, in the form of symbolical puppets, and, in so doing, to enhance his own importance as a creator, the creator-hero of the Cervantine novel of his own life and his own fictitious world.

In the *esperpento* entitled *Los cuernos de don Friolera*, in reference to Compadre Fidel, the sole owner, director and actor of a puppet show, the character Don Estrafalario says: "That Puppeteer does not for a single moment cease to think of himself as superior by nature to the puppets in his show. He has a demiurgic dignity."[34] And in a conversation between the same character and Don Manolito, we read:

> *Don Manolito.*—We have to love, Don Estrafalario: laughter and tears are the paths of God. This is my esthetics, and yours.
> *Don Estrafalario.*—No, not mine. My esthetics is a transcending of pain and laughter, something like the conversations of the dead, when they tell each other stories about the living.
>
> . . . .
>
> *Don Manolito.*—You, Don Estrafalario, you want to be like God!
> *Don Estrafalario.*—I would like to see this world with the perspective of the other shore. I am like that relative of mine that you have met, who, on one occasion, when the political boss asked him what he would like to be appointed, answered: Me, deceased.[35]

In this dialogue Don Estrafalario is the one that articulates the opinions of the author, as of that date, that is to say, the esthetics of the *esperpento*, whereas Don Manolito embodies that of the preceding humorous and ironical period, which is represented by Valle-Inclán's farces.

The question of the "required" lack of identification of the satirist with his country and his countrymen, will appear more convincing and much less controversial in Valle-Inclán's case if we remember that he identified his intimate self with his Galician—not Castilian—background and origin, although they were both subjected by him to a constant literary idealization. He preferred to think of himself as a man of the geographical and cultural periphery—the traditional center being Castile—and of Galicia as much more akin to the Basque provinces and other regions facing the Bay of Biscay, and much less to the rest of the Iberian peninsula.[36]

As a first general conclusion, it is perhaps reasonable to say that the *esperpento* resulted from a satirical approach to reality, to the reality of a modern Spanish society permeated with traditional values that were felt to be in crisis, not only in Spanish life but throughout Western and perhaps even universal culture. But even if we may agree on this, we still do not have an answer to the more fundamental question of what the characteristics, the nature and the artistic value are of the created *reality* that we know as the *esperpento.*

Valle-Inclán applied the word *esperpento* to one of his creations for the first time immediately after the First World War, and literary critics have unanimously recognized that Valle-Inclán's whole production thereafter responded, in the main, to a *visión esperpéntica* of the Spanish-speaking world from those days back to approximately the middle of the XIXth century. There is the possibility of a Valle-Inclán *Weltanschauung* and the indisputable fact of a new novelistic dimension called the *esperpento.* Specifically, only three separate books were so entitled by Valle-Inclán himself: *Luces de Bohemia* (1920), *Los cuernos de don Friolera* (1921), and *La hija del capitán* (1927). He added to the group a fourth title, the *Esperpento de las galas del difunto*, which he included with the last two (excluding *Luces de Bohemia*) in a single volume entitled *Martes de carnaval: Esperpentos* (1930). *The Esperpento de las galas del difunto*, had appeared earlier as *El terno del difunto: Novela* (1926). The word *novela* in the title indicates perhaps that the author did not consider this work a clear example of the new genre.[37] The other three, nevertheless, offer enough common elements on which to base an analysis and a possible characterization. Among these elements are: the selection and treatment of personages; the lack of a linear, forward-developing plot; the emphasis on the possibility of what I would call a recurrent present; and, finally and most importantly, a self-sufficient objectivity.

In regard to personages, *Luces de Bohemia* brings into focus a gallery of alienated human beings—as alienated as the author himself—, most, if not all, of them known as real persons in the "outside world" (the physical world) by the author, the author's friends, and even some of his readers. The situation is repeated in the "inside world" of the book itself, where they all intermingle to illustrate a side of human society not recognized as valuable by "normal" people, or by those occupied in normal and respectable activities. The author appears in the work *hidden* as the third-person narrator, apparently responsible only for the equivalent of stage directions; and he appears also *in the open* but in a marginal capacity, disguised as an idealized *alter ego. Los cuernos de don Friolera* placed together, in a much more structurally complex pattern, another disguised *alter ego* of the real author, accompanied by a transfiguration of one of his closest friends in real life,[38] and both of them appear in the same alienated or marginal capacity, while the author takes care also of his narrator role. The three of them—the narrator and the two marginal characters—view from the fictitious outside a presentation of a single problem—the sempiternal Spanish case of *honor* on three different levels. Underlying all three, there is also an actual happening in the outside contemporary world, with identifiable disguised persons, and others mentioned by their real names.[39] *La hija del capitán* lacks the marginal appearance of any direct or disguised *alter ego* of the author. All fictional pretenses are put aside and the author plays, in a demiurgic manner, his role as the *hidden* but identifiable narrator. In this case, he seems to prefer not to get close to his characters, to keep his distance, motivated perhaps by a mixed feeling of pride and disgust in regard to the type of puppets he is manipulating. This *esperpento* coincides, nevertheless, with the other two in also being an artistic re-elaboration of a recent actual happening, in this particular case a big historical event: the *pronunciamiento* of General Primo de Rivera (1923), in connivance with King Alfonso XIII, both of whom appear in the book, along with other recognizable and historical figures, as *Un general glorioso* and *El monarca*, respectively.

The fact that most of the personages in the *esperpentos*, have one foot in the outside or physical world, and are what might be called "newspaper character," makes any detailed description of them unnecessary. They are already present, full-length, in the imagination of potential readers, and especially in the imagination of the author himself. Their substance derives from memory, the author's and the reader's. Emerging from memory they enter, through the written page, an imaginary stage ready to play the role assigned to them by the author, and if they become real within the *esperpento*, it will be with the reality of the puppet—not that of the human being and not even that of the actor in the legitimate theater. They lack all signs of the *duality* characteristic of living human beings and of the *duality* inherent in the characters of the traditional novel. And as puppets, they are not supposed to have real souls. They belong to the same family of stylized symbolical figures which in the past had populated the multiple stages of the *moralidades* and *autos sacramentales*, although the similarity ends there. They *are* what they *seem to be* or they *seem to be* what they *are*. They have entered the stage with the appropriate make-up on, leaving behind their original dual nature as characters from life and/or from fiction. In life and in fiction one could always become something else, and as a last recourse it was even possible to become the object of one's own knowledge. But in the *esperpento*, the personage *is* what he *is*, his being coinciding with what the author wants him to be, which is mainly the incarnation of an *essential negative trait*, unmoved and unchangeable, acting against a background of degraded personal and social values and before the "conscience" of the reader-spectator. All the personages that Valle-Inclán brought from life, from memory, from literature into the written word he brought already *crystallized*, selecting for the *esperpentos* those whose *essence* (or being) had appeared to him pre-determined by an unauthentic *existence* ("cowards" or "misfits" in the terminology of Sartre).

If the characters can not evolve, if they can not change for better or worse, it is only logical to deduce that the use of motivation and action by the author will be superfluous. In *Luces de Bohemia* this use is limited to Max and Don Latino walking the streets of Madrid, after leaving Max's house, ostensibly to redeem the books they have pawned for three *pesetas.* And already in the very first scene, Claudinita announced that the whole thing will end in the tavern of Pica Lagartos, which is precisely what happens later. Between beginning and end, some things happen to the personages, but mainly we and they are limited to the sharing of different and disconnected experiences. The emphasis is on the receptive and not on the active mood, with the interest of the superficial reader kept alive only by the picturesque aspects of Bohemian life, very lightly put together in a total of fifteen *cuadros* (the author calls them *scenes*), which are full of plasticity and each almost autonomous. *Los cuernos de don Friolera* gives us, in a total of fourteen *cuadros* (one less than *Luces de Bohemia*), an old and recurrent story in a triple perspective re-elaborated in three different mediums: the puppet show, the theater, and the ballad, in that order. The puppet show is included in a sort of *prologue*, and the ballad in a kind of *epilogue.* But it would not be too illogical to assume that the germinal inspiration—for the theatrical version, at least—could have been a real happening immediately structured in the ballad. Therefore, the content of the *epilogue* ought chronologically to occupy the first place, and not the last, while that of the prologue might very well be the real *epilogue.* This juggling with natural order can be interpreted as a functional disregard for the plot itself, which, on the other hand, is presented here in this sort of superimposed or coincidental structures in order to underline the differences in treatment. *La hija del capitán* is the shortest of these three *esperpentos*, barely one-third the length of *Luces de*

Bohemia and approximately one-half that of *Los cuernos de don Friolera*, but its content is, comparatively speaking, even more subdivided, in a total of seven *cuadros.* The plot, melodramatic and anecdotal, is a pretext to show the reader, retrospectively, the moral and intellectual caliber of the military men responsible for the dictatorship under which the country was suffering. Most of the actions of the characters are either incidental or totally irrelevant to the *coup d'état* itself.

The fragmentation of contents, unchangeable nature of the personages, and lack of sustained plots, which we have seen in all three of these *esperpentos*, are clear signs of a tendency on the part of the author to paralyze or, at least, to retard and even reverse the flow of chronological time. A closer look at the treatment of time in these works will show a marked preference for human time in opposition to external or clock time.

Luces de Bohemia begins at an abstract "twilight hour" of a certain day. Twelve *cuadros later*, at dawn of the following morning, the main character, Max Estrella, will die. Only three more *cuadros* are left, which we may reasonably guess, take place a couple of days later. On another level, and in contrast to the allusion to the recent death of Don Benito el Garbancero (referring to Galdós who died in 1920, the very year of the publication of this *esperpento*), is the appearance, as living characters, of others long since dead, such as, for example, Rubén Darío. *Los cuernos de don Friolera* also begins on an unidentified "morning". A conversation between Don Manolito and Don Estrafalario serves—as we have seen previously—as a *prologue* to the story of Don Friolera, which by clock time logically precedes the conversation between the two characters. In the *prologue* we have already seen Don Manolito and Don Estrafalario as spectators of the puppet version of the story of Don Friolera. The space-time sequence of the actual story is predominantly indicated in an indirect way, by expressions such as: "What have you done this morning, Don Manolito?" or "The orchard of

Don Friolera at sunset" or "Nocturnal bright stars framed by the little window." The historical present is nevertheless very much in evidence, with references to the bullfighter Belmonte, to the last Kaiser, to the assassination of the Spanish premier Dato, to the actress María Guerrero, etc. *La hija del capitán* starts with the mention of a "siesta" hour and continues with the same type of indirect reference to the night of a second day. Only the events of the last *cuadro* take place, independently, several days later, and since they are made up of recent political happenings of national importance, the reader is able to locate them in chronological historical time, while artistically they are given to him in an ahistorical present. This *esperpento* offers also a very eloquent example of consciousness of human time on the part of the author and of its functional use within the work itself. This occurs at the end of the second scene. Pollo de Cartagena has just been killed and his last cry has been heard. Valle-Inclán comments:

> The anguished echo of that shout paralyzes the gestures of the three figures, suspending their actions: They are imprisoned in a livid fracture in time, that prolongs the instant, and fills it with dramatic uncertainty.[40]

In that prolonged instant the author places a dialogue between two characters, some action, the end of one scene, and the beginning of another, with the result that literary time becomes of much longer duration than clock time.

To Valle-Inclán's exclusive use of a few hours or a few days as a time limit in the *esperpentos*, there may be added still other devices tending to the paralization of time, such as: the almost exclusive use of dialogue in order to establish the interrelationships of characters presented to the reader-spectator; the predominant use of the present tense; the frequency of the simple nouns, nouns in apposition, and nominal syntagmas, especially in the descriptions; and a few others. Valle-Inclán's constant tendency was, indeed, to eliminate the past and the future and to make the present a vehicle for real atemporality.

It would be deceiving to consider national raw materials, as used by Valle-Inclán in the elaboration of the *esperpento*, as a *sine qua non* of its existence and, in consequence, to regard the *esperpento* as an exclusively Spanish product. One thing is what reality offers—more or less the same all over—and another is what man does with it. The peculiarities of Spanish life during the last hundred years have—unfortunately, let us add—become a possibility in all countries and are already a matter of fact in many of them. The crisis of traditional values and the discrepancy between the inner "being" and the public "image" in society's contemporary representatives is too obvious for anyone not to see. But what Spain did with its own *circumstances*—in this case through the genius of Valle-Inclán—was to play once more a pioneering role in the transformation of an aspect of the amorphous human reality into a meaningful artistic formula. Don Estrafalario undoubtedly succeeded in his wish to see "this world with the perspective of the other shore". And Valle-Inclán—Don Estrafalario's *alter ego* in life—after many years of self-discipline and preparation took into account what Don Estrafalario saw and remade it into an independent and self-sufficient objectivity, of which a few fragments newly put together have become known as *esperpentos.* But these—I submit before concluding—are neither the result of deformation nor of stylization of a given reality, as has been said and repeated many times. To consider the *esperpentos* as deformed reality would imply a contradiction in terms, and for them to be a stylization would require a pre-existent pattern or model to serve as a basis. The *esperpentos* are new artistic structures, formed—or conformed—according to a new concept and a new vision of reality. The whole range of their ingredients, including even the language itself, has been reduced to *essence*—the phenomenological *eidos*—and they "realize" themselves with their action taking place not in any kind of "outside" location, but in the individual who is participating, consciously or subconsciously, in the predominant spiritual situation of his time. The way toward the *esperpento* was prepared by a complex process of disrealization, which culminated in artistic autonomy for the resultant product and a complete break with the procedures used in the novelistic art of the period that preceded it. Its masterpiece is *Tirano Banderas* (1925–1926), which has all the *esperpentic* characteristics of the others, but which Valle-Inclán chose not to call an *esperpento* but a *novela*, as if to confirm that he was by that time satisfied with his discovery of this new dimension for the old genre.

NOTES

[1] See the drawing of Valle-Inclán published in *El País Gallego* (Santiago de Compostela, 1891), reproduced in my book A *Bibliography and Iconography of Valle-Inclán (1866–1936)*, [Berkeley and Los Angeles: University of California Press, 1960], p. 65.

[2] "En las tranquilas calles de Pontevedra su presencia tuvo la importancia de un insólito acontecimiento. Su extraño empaque llenó de conturbación el ánimo socarrón de las comadres y desafió las facecias de las gentes sin que hacer." Joaquín Pesqueira, "Don Ramón del Valle-Inclán," *El Correo Gallego* (El Ferrol), January 12, 1936.

[3]. . . "la altiva y extravagante prestancia de aquel hombre menudo" . . . *Ibidem.*

[4] *Ibidem.*

[5] The *Diccionario de la lengua española* of the Real Academia did not include the term *esperpento* until the 1914 edition, where it appears thus: "Esperpento. m. fam. Persona rara ridícula || 2. Desatino, absurdo." Later editions changed the first definition to: "persona o cosa notable por su fealdad, desaliño o mala traza." Previously the word had appeared in Eduardo Benot's *Diccionario de ideas afines,* under *payasería,* with *visión*" and "*pendón*", as synonyms. It had also been included in the *Diccionario de la lengua castellana* (Paris: Garnier [1911]) by Zerolo, de Toro, Isaza, *et al.*, with the definition: "Persona fea, extravagante y de aspecto ridículo." The complete history and etymology of the word are unknown. Joan Corominas, in his *Diccionario crítico etimológico de la lengua castellana* (Madrid: Gredos, 1954), after giving as the meaning of the word "persona o cosa muy fea, desatino literario," labels it "palabra familiar y reciente de origen incierto." Of the suggesions made by Professor Corominas regarding its etymology, the

most plausible points to a possible crossing of the Italian words *spavento* and *spérpero.*

[6] "estaba sentado un joven barbudo, melenudo, moreno, flaco hasta la momificación. Vestía de negro; se cubría la cabeza con chambergo de felpa grisácea, de alta copa cónica y ancha ala. Las puntas enhiestas del almidonado cuello de la camisa avanzaban amenazadoras, flanqueando la negrísima barba, cortada a la moda ninivita del siglo XIX antes de la Era Cristiana. Bajo la barba se adivinaba apenas la flotante chalina de seda negra. ¡Tan cara a los espíritus románticos!

No me atrevía a contemplarle fijamente. El extraño personaje respondía a las curiosas miradas de los concurrentes del café con aire desfachatado e insultante y dirigía el destello de sus quevedos, que cabalgaban sobre su larga nariz contra quien le mirara con insistencia." Ricardo Baroja, *Gente del 98* (Madrid: Juventud, 1952), p. 16.

[7] . . . "la mejor máscara a pie que cruzaba la calle de Alcalá, y yo recuerdo haberle visto pasar tieso, orgulloso, pero ocultándose de vez en cuando detrás de las carteleras de los toros, que eran como burladeros contra las cornadas de aquel público que le llama 'el poeta melenudo.' " *Ramón Gómez* de la Serna, *Don Ramón María del Valle Inclán* (Buenos Aires-México: Espasa Calpe Argentina, 1944) p. 26.

[8] "Vivió casi exclusivamente para esa tarea [to be a *divo*]. Usó todos los reclamos imaginables. Y físicamente era ya una especie de cartel de propaganda, mediante aquella figura que supo componerse a fuerza de talento teatral, con aquellas barbas inverosímiles, aquellas gafas impresionantes, y después sus fantasías, sus salidas de tono, sus paradojas e intemperancias; su modo de estar en el café y en la calle como un histrión fantástico que convierte la vida en escena, y él quiere ser el único protagonista." José Ma. Salaverría, "Paralelismo literario," *ABC* (Madrid), March 9, 1936.

[9] "! ! Sí! ! ! ! El poeta debe ser un hombre absurdo! !" Manuel Azaña, "Mi amigo Valle-Inclán," *La Pluma* (Madrid), IV, 32 (1923), p. 87.

[10] . . . "un semidiós movido por el afán de la justicia absoluta. Sus odios, su crueldad verbal, su intransigencia, pueden invocar, en el origen, un motivo de interés público aceptable. Es un héroe desprovisto de misericordia, que ha tirado muchas piedras porque estaba libre de pecado. Se sitúa naturalmente en la extrema oposición. Es una picota de lo mediocre y de lo malo; un anticipo del juicio final para chirles, los hipócritas, los vividores; es un hurón que vocifera sus despegos. Pero esa justicia, que ama tanto, no la aprende en otros, ni menos la recibe de una ley exterior. Valle-Inclán es el hombre de la ley propia, que desprecia la jerarquía social y legal *porque está corrompida." Ibidem.*

[11] "Es seguro que ni en París, ni en Berlín, ni en Londres, ni en Nueva York se ha visto en los tiempos modernos nada semejante a Valle-Inclán." Ramiro de Maeztu, "Valle-Inclán," *ABC* (Madrid), January 8, 1936.

[12] This attitude also corresponds to the ethics of the artist, as understood by many XIXth-century creators. Gustave Flaubert, for instance, speaking about himself, says: "I am leading a stern existence, stripped of all external pleasure, and am sustained only by a kind of permanent rage, which sometimes makes me weep tears of impotence but which never abates. I love my work with a love that is frenzied and perverted, as an ascetic loves the hair shirt that scratches his belly." Gustave Flaubert, Letter to Louise Colet [1852], in *Selected Letters*, tr. from the French by Francis Steegmuller, London, 1954, p. 131.

[13] "¿Qué había en la espalda de sus invectivas, de sus clamorosas indignaciones? Había, sin duda, un muy cerrado y estricto sistema de valores morales y culturales."

"Entonces parecía un extremado negador, un anacrónico anarquista y, en realidad, era solamente un *outsider*, un desplazado, un marginal. Un hombre que está y no está en el mundo circundante. Que *entiende* y no *participa*. Y porque entiende *juzga*. Y porque juzga, *condena*." D. García-Sabell, "Españoles mal entendidos. II. Don Ramón del Valle-Inclán," *Insula*, (Madrid), XVI (July–August, 1961).

[14] . . . "Y ya en trance de morirse, yo tenía en mis manos una nota escrita apresuradamente a lápiz y en la que D. Ramón decía: "Venga a verme. Vuelven los terribles dolores y *estoy a punto de quejarme como una mujer*." Ahora las circunstancias eran reales, ferozmente reales—un tumor corroyéndole las entrañas—y la reacción, varonil, temerosa, permitía entrever la veta estoica, fabricada y acatada a un tiempo, del gran escritor. Ahora D. Ramón hacía pie, tocaba fondo en el mundo y, con todo, seguía, obediente, el imperativo de unos mandatos ideales, esquemáticos, literarios." *Ibidem.*

[15] For an understanding of what I mean by the term "Cervantine novel," see my essay: "Alonso Quijano y Don Quijote. Reflexiones sobre el "ser" de la novela." *Cuadernos* (Paris), 47 (March–April 1961).

[16] The word *esperpento* applied to a literary work may have occurred first in Spanish America, and probably in Mexico, and Valle-Inclán may have become familiar with such a meaning in his travels and in his readings of Spanish American authors and vocabularies. For instance, in the *Vocabulario de mexicanismos* (México: J. Aguilar Vera y Comp., 1905) by Joaquín García Icazbalceta, the word is entered as follows: "Esperpento. m. Persona o cosa vieja, mal pergeñada, extravagante, que de fea pone espanto. Aplicado a piezas teatrales, *culebrón*." Under the word *culebrón*, we find: "Nombre burlesco que se da a una pieza de teatro disparatada, particularmente si se ha buscado en ella el efecto por medio de incidentes estrepitosos y escenas truculentas." García Icazbalceta illustrates the use of both words with the following text from the book *Isolina la ex-figurante* by Facundo [José Tomás de Cuéllar], (México: Ignacio Cumplido, 1871, pp. 94–95): "Al paso que, continuó María, el mismo público quedó encantado con una

pieza del teatro francés que es un *esperpento.*/ / — ¿Un qué?/ /—Un esperpento./ / — Perdóneme usted, señorita, nosotros los que no vivimos en las ciudades, no entendemos muchos términos de esos . . . ¿cómo decía Ud? ¿un qué?/ / — Un esperpento, o lo que es lo mismo, un culebrón./ / — ¿Esperpento es lo mismo que culebrón?/ / —Sí señor./ / —Y culebrón y esperpento quieren decir . . ./ / — Una comedia mala. (Facundo, *Isolina,* tomo I, cap. 7)."

[17] It may be pertinent to recall that in no other European country did there exist, to the same degree as is Spain, the possibility of a double life, owing to the social need of a great part of the population to hide Islamic or Jewish beliefs. This was undoubtedly a vital factor favoring the creation of the novel.

[18] "So profound, moreover, and lasting is this our intrinsic dualism and duplicity—(and I use the term here, not in its usual moral sense, but in a higher signification, which is purely psychological and metaphysical)—so deeply is this dualism rooted in our consciousness, that even when we are, or at least think ourselves alone, we will think as two, and are constrained as it were to recognize our inmost profoundest being as essentially dramatic." Friedrich Schlegel, *The Philosophy of Life and the Philosophy of Language,* tr. from the German by A. J. Morrison (London, 1847), p. 389.

[19] . . . "la *epoché* consiste en no entregarse al objeto o a la proposición; en no vivir el acto correspondiente, sino en considerarlo o contemplarlo refleja y puramente, tomando el objeto o la proposición como meramente intencionales o presentes, absteniéndonos de compartir la tesis, de consentir en ningún juicio sobre la realidad del objeto o sobre la verdad de la proposición." José Gaos, *Introducción a la Fenomenología, seguida de la Crítica del Psicologismo en Husserl,* (México: Universidad Veracruzana, 1960), p. 67.

[20] It is very revealing that even the title *The Picaresque Saint of* R.W.B. Lewis's excellent book on contemporary fiction, contains an allusion to an old Spanish literary creation, and that he writes: "For contemporary fiction, even while it is attempting to remodel the distracted world it deals with, is returning to the sources of the narrative tradition to find the means to do so. The episodic novel, the tale of successive encounters, the paradoxical hero and his ambiguous relation to the world he travels through: all these elements which characterize the second generation [i.e., the generation of writers like Silone, Camus, Faulkner, Moravia, Greene and Malraux; which followed that of Joyce, Proust and Mann] are at least as old as the work which is usually taken as the chief ancestor of modern prose fiction in general—*Don Quixote.*" *The Picaresque Saint* (Philadelphia and New York: J. B. Lippincott, 1961) pp. 294–295.

[21] "¡Grotescas horas españolas en que todo suena a moneda fullera! Todos los valores tienen hoja—la Historia, la Política, las Armas, las Academias—.

Nunca había sido tan mercantilista la que entonces comenzó a llamarse Gran Prensa—G.P.—. ¡Maleante sugestión tiene el anagrama!"

. . . .

"Ajenos a la vida española, sin una sola atadura por donde recibir provecho, hemos visto con una mirada de buen humor treinta años de historia." Ricardo Baroja, *El Pedigree* (Madrid: Caro Raggio, [1926]), p. 11. *El Pedigree* had been previously published in the pages of the *Revista de Occidente,* in 1924, and had appeared two years later in book form, with slight changes and the preface by Valle-Inclán.

[22] "Con estas regocijadas memorias no intento significar que haya mudanza en los tiempos. Son más vistosos que nunca los plumajes y las bandas, los discursos y los alboroques de las gloriosas retiradas. La consecuencia es virtud española, y cuando parece trastocada la mojiganga es porque aumenta el número de los babiones." *Ibidem, p. 12.*

[23] "Y ya dentro de mi alma, rosa obstinada, me río de todo lo divino y de todo lo humano y no creo mas que en la belleza." Quoted by Guillermo Díaz-Plaja, *Modernismo frente a Noventa y ocho* (Madrid: Espasa-Calpe, 1951), p. 76.

[24] "No fumo, no bebo vino, odio el café y los toros, la religión y el militarismo, el acordeón y la pena de muerte," *Ibidem,* p. 77.

[25] See R.W.B. Lewis, *op. cit.,* p. 298, note 11. Quoted from a letter (in English) to Mr. Lewis by Alberto Moravia.

[26] From an interview with C. Rivas Cherif in *El Sol* (Madrid), September 3, 1920.

[27] "La Dirección General de Seguridad, Cumpliendo órdenes del Gobierno, ha dispuesto la recogida de un folleto, titulado *La hija del Capitán,* cuya publicación califica su autor de "esperpento," no habiendo en aquél renglón qué no hiera el buen gusto ni omita denigrar a clases respetabilísimas a través de la más absurda de las fábulas. Si pudiera darse a la luz pública algún trozo del mencionado folleto, sería suficiente para poner de manifiesto que la determinación administrativa no está inspirada en un criterio estrecho e intolerable y sí exclusivamente en el de impedir la circulación de aquellos escritos que sólo pueden alcanzar el resultado de prostituir el gusto, atentando a las buenas costumbres." Reprinted by Francisco Madrid, *op. cit.,* p. 71.

[28] Signed by C.R.C., almost surely the initials of Cipriano Rivas Cherif, a theatrical critic and personal friend of Valle-Inclán, there appeared in the review *España* (Madrid), December 29, 1923, p. 10, the following commentary: "Al día siguiente, dispuso muy acertadamente [Dario] Niccodemi la representación de *La maschera e il volto* de Luigi Chiarelli, crítico teatral *antes que fraile* [underlined in the original] e iniciador a lo que parece de la franca evolución hacia el humorismo, característica de las nuevas tendencias del teatro italiano."

. . . .

"Tiene acento inglés. La fábula, por lo demás, se parece harto a otros modelos del mismo problema, planteado con patética gravedad en *El cadáver vivo* de Tolstoi; con una gracia ya muy próxima a la de Chiarelli por Arnold Bennett; y casi en los mismos términos en *El farsante del mundo occidental* del irlandés Synge."

[29] "También ha dado lugar el eximio escritor y extravagante ciudadano señor Valle-Inclán a la determinación de su arresto, porque al negarse a satisfacer la multa de 250 pesetas que se le había impuesto por infracción gubernativa, con el ánimo de evitarle privaciones de la libertad, ha proferido contra la autoridad tales insultos y contra el orden social establecido ataques tan demoledores que se ha hecho imposible eximirle de sanción como era el propósito . . ." M. Fernández Almagro, *Vida y literatura de Valle-Inclán* (Madrid: Nacional, 1943), p. 233.

[30] "L'humour ne veut pas blesser, ni même trop critiquer, mais surtout amuser. Voulant enlever á ses procédés tout caractére agressif, l'humouriste ne se borne pas à dégrader légérement les valeurs d'autrui, mais aussi celles qui lui sont propres. Il permet qu'on rie à ses dépens, avouant ceci: 'Je ne suis pas meilleur que les autres, je ne suis pas non plus une exception' "

. . . .

. . . "l'humour crée donc un lien entre les hommes, tandis que la satire les sépare les uns des autres." Alfred Stern, *Philosophie du rire et des pleurs* (Paris: Presses Universitaires de France, 1949), p. 133; 134.

[31] . . . "montrent qu'il est plus qu'un jeu accompagnant la vie. *L'art* est une partie même de la vie, son *aspect axiologique idéal." Ibidem,* p. 236.

[32] . . . "*si la satire cherche a dégrader les valeurs collectives d'un certain groupe ou les valeurs individuelles d'un certain sujet, c'est pour faire triompher finalement les valeurs universelles de l'humanité,* qui ont été supplantées ou offusquées par des valeurs collectives ou individuelles. En dernier lieu, la satire est donc capable d'unir les humains sur un *plan supérieur,* le plan des valeurs universelles" . . . *Ibidem,* p. 242.

[33] "El ayuno del estilista es de pasiones y de ambiciones de todas las cosas del mundo" . . .

. . . .

. . . "El artista debe mirar el paisaje con "ojos de altura" para poder abarcar todo el conjunto y no los detalles mudables."

. . . .

. . . "hay que pintar a las figuras añadiéndoles aquello que no hayan sido. Así un mendigo debe parecerse a Job y un guerrero a Aquiles." Quoted by Ramón Gómez de la Serna, *op. cit.,* pp. 109–110.

[34] . . . "ese Bululú, ni un solo momento deja de considerarse superior por naturaleza, a los muñecos de su tabanque. Tiene una dignidad demiúrgica."

Obras completas, vol. II (Madrid: Rivadeneyra, 1944), p. 1706. In subsequent references to this volume the abbreviation *O.C. II* is used.

[35] *Don Manolito.*—Hay que amar, Don Estrafalario: La risa y las lágrimas son los caminos de Dios. Esa es mi estética, y la de usted.

Don Estrafalario.—La mía no. Mi estética es una superación del dolor y de la risa, como deben ser las conversaciones de los muertos, al contarse historias de los vivos.

. . . .

Don Manolito.—¡Usted, Don Estrafalario quiere ser como Dios!

Don Estrafalario.—Yo quisiera ver este mundo con la perspectiva de la otra ribera. Soy como aquel mi pariente que usted conoció, y que una vez, al preguntarle el cacique, qué deseaba ser, contestó: Yo, difunto. *O.C. II,* pp. 1698; 1699.

[36] "Castilla está muerta, porque Castilla vive mirando atrás, y mirando atrás, no se tiene una visión del momento."

. . . .

"Pero el pueblo vasco, y con el pueblo vasco todos los que se asoman al Cantábrico, no se han desenvuelto aún, no pueden mirar atrás, a un anterior, a una época anterior, a unas conquistas y a una historia geográfica, y siempre pasada como toda la historia, ni tienen tampoco una ciencia aprendida de ajenos; son primitivos." From a commentary of Valle-Inclán, included with others by Ortega, Unamuno, Sánchez Mazas, etc. in the book: *La pintura vasca,* 1909–1919: *Antología* (Madrid: Hernández, 1919), pp. 6–7.

[37] Another possible explanation is that, as happened on other occasions, the editor wanted more material to increase the size of the volume, which, without the already published *Luces de Bohemia,* would perhaps have been too short. The fact that this work was placed first in the volume may also carry an implication of its introductory nature.

[38] Don Manolito el Pintor reflects Ricardo Baroja the painter, and Don Estrafalario is the disguised *alter ego* of Valle-Inclán himself.

[39] "Pero donde [Valle-Inclán] pone más pimienta, aunque sí más (*sic*) tranquilidad y regocijo, es hablando de los militares. Nos dice, de cómo por culpa de la ley de jurisdicciones, tuvo que valerse de su ingenio para escribir sobre ellos en una forma y estilo nuevo, (*sic*) a la medida, que podríamos llamar. Nos explica cómo en sentido figurado hizo una historia de un *Teniente Friolera,* y para cuya historia echó mano del bello romance, ya en desuso—que nos recitó—y por cuyo motivo los militares estaban dispuestos a hacerle una encerrona. La *providencia* vino en su auxilio. Un caso exactamente igual al del *Teniente Friolera* sucedió en Madrid, y no hubo más remedio que acatar a Don Ramón." Mario López Bacelo, "Una visita a Valle-Inclán," *España Nueva* (La Habana), November 30, 1921, p. 53.

[40] "El eco angustiado de aquel grito paraliza el gesto de las tres figuras, suspende su acción: Quedan aprisionadas en una desgarradura lívida del tiempo, que alarga el instante y lo colma de dramática incertidumbre." *O.C. II,* p. 1829.

JOSÉ LUIS CANO

VALLE-INCLÁN AND CONTEMPORARY SPAIN

Translated by

JOSÉ SÁNCHEZ

On the fourteenth of February, 1936, now over thirty years ago, I attended in Madrid a celebration in honor of Ramón del Valle-Inclán. The event took place in the Teatro de la Zarzuela, and it was organized by the Ateneo de Madrid. Some poets of the so-called Generation of 1927 took active part in that event. Thus they manifested their admiration for the great writer who had just died. I remember Federico García Lorca reciting Rubén Darío's "Soneto autumnal" and also the prologue to *Voces de gesta*; Luis Cernuda reading Juan Ramón Jiménez' admirable essay, "Ramón del Valle-Inclán (Castillo de Quema)," published weeks earlier by the daily *El Sol;* Rafael Alberti as he read the prose from *Juan de Mairena* which referred to Don Ramón and which also appeared in *El Sol*. And finally, I remember Francisco Vighi telling with unique gracefulness some anecdotes about Valle-Inclán. The second part of the celebration consisted of a staging of *Los cuernos de don Friolera*, giving thus the celebration a certain political flavor because of the antimilitarism expressed in the work. Madrid was then burning in its fight for the Popular Front and four days later, on the eighteenth of February, the political parties of the left won the elections in Spain and assumed power.[1]

The Teatro de la Zarzuela event was the Spanish Left's homage to the independent writer, to the gentlemen "free of beggary and envy" who was Valle-Inclán, as Antonio Machado put it. To be sure, the celebration had begun even before, on the day following the great writer's death. In an article entitled "Valle-Inclán visto por sus coetáneos," published in the review *Indice Literario,*[2] Pedro Salinas gathered some opinions expressed by writers of the Generation of 1898 about the character and works of Valle-Inclán. These opinions had appeared in the Madrid press during the days after Don Ramón's death, and were, to be specific, those of Benavente, Unamuno, Azorín, Baroja, Maeztu, Manuel Bueno, and Juan Ramón Jiménez. Of these opinions, no doubt the most interesting are Unamuno's, Benavente's, and Juan Ramón Jiménez'. I shall not quote them here. It would be impossible, on the other hand, to summarize some of those texts and especially that small masterpiece of evocative prose which is Jiménez' "Ramón del Valle-Inclán (Castillo de Quema)" published in *El Sol* on the twenty-sixth of January. As Pedro Salinas says, it is both "a personal portrait and that of an epoch, of the most luminous and rich that he [J.R.J.] has written."

In his article, Salinas gathered only the opinions held by Valle-Inclán's fellow members of the Generation of 1898. But what about the writers of the following generations? From among the hundreds of articles published in the Madrid press and reviews on the occasion of Valle-Inclán's death, I have gathered the opinions of some intellectuals of two generations: that of 1914, to which Ortega belongs; and the Generation of 1927. The first of these was more politically minded than that of 1898, and included, among others, Manuel Azaña, Antonio Espina, José Bergamín, Corpus Barga, Benjamín Jarnés, Juan del Encina, José Díaz Fernández, and Rafael Cansinos-Asséns. Let me begin by citing Pedro Salinas' text, which, as far as I know, has never been reprinted:

> Valle-Inclán found unity only in his extremes. Led astray by the initial phase of his work, critics thought he was only a delicate artist, a painter of miniatures. But the real Valle-Inclán is rather the writer who treats barbarous themes with refinement, who stylizes violence. Crude human nature is violence, barbarity. And words are the divine power which elevates it to the quality of art. The art-process in Valle-Inclán, who always scoffed at the reality of the realist, lies in passing through a stylization of the real, concerned above all with the aesthetic, such as in the *Sonatas,* to another kind of stylization—mystic and profound—which we might call a stylization of psychological origin. At first he proceeded inwardly and dressed his characters in artistically designed costumes taken from literature and painting. But in his last period the characters emit from within themselves their own elements of stylization as they become their own caricature; and what accounts for the tragic element in the *esperpento* is precisely man's encounter with his own acts, with his own farce and grimace. He converts himself into a tragicomic motif as he encounters his own true character. At the beginning of his career Valle-Inclán may have indeed been a sensual contemplator and a sceptic, but in the end he is a man in anguish, and in his works, what he gives us is a plastic transcription—for Valle-Inclán could never be anything if not plastic—of man's confiict with his conscience.

These lines are perhaps embryonic of the essay Salinas published years later under the title "Significación del esperpento o Valle, hijo pródigo del '98."

Another member of the generation of 1927, Juan José Domenchina, wrote the following:

> Tears on the death of Valle-Inclán? No. The creator of Malpocado was a complete man. Out of his spirited temper and his disdain for and animosity toward the academic, we derive a clear, luminous lesson. Valle-Inclán is not to be mourned. He ought to be read as a writer and imitated as a man, if our heart's courage allows it.[3]

Among the texts written by political men the most interesting are those of Manuel Azaña, who was very close to Valle-Inclán, Fernando de los Ríos, and Indalecio Prieto. Azaña's article was published in *Política*, his party's voice, on the seventh of January, 1936. Wrote Azaña:

> On his open tomb, all we can do is bid him farewell. Some months back we attended a funeral together in Madrid, and as we crossed the patio—dilapidated in the extreme—of an old cemetery, Don Ramón said to me: 'What a fine place to rot, in such peacefulness.' Now he is dead. For years he had settled with death, and now he has confronted it as he lived: whole, chimerical, and poor.

I shall also mention a biographical note from the article by Fernando de los Ríos:

> The last twenty years in the life of Valle-Inclán gradually gave his political preoccupation a more human tone and a greater protest value against all injustice. The events which took place in 1934 [the repressive measure taken against the revolt of the Asturian miners] so moved Valle-Inclán that they made his eloquence, rich and fluent, produce the most beautiful imprecations, which those of us who heard them shall never forget.[4]

It is evident, from these opinions, that the work and character of Valle-Inclán provoked the enthusiastic admiration of leftist groups, those who had fought on the side of the Republic and the greater part of whom left in exile when the Civil War ended. The adherence of the Spanish Left to what Valle-Inclán represented as a person and literary figure gained in intensity, given Valle-Inclán's position following the dictatorship of Primo de Rivera in the twenties. On the other hand, the Spanish Right could not forgive Don Ramón, at the moment of the tense political struggle on the eve of the Popular Front, his anticlerical and antimonarchic outbursts, his mordant scoffing of militarism —as in *Los cuernos de don Friolera* and *La hija del capitán*, for instance—and especially his adherence to the Asociación de Amigos de la Unión Soviética and to the Congreso para la Defensa de la Cultura, both clearly of revolutionary inspiration. The Spanish monarchists never forgave him his ridiculing portrait of Isabel II in the *Ruedo ibérico* novels and in the *Farsa y licencia de la reina castiza*, nor his effrontery toward King Alfonso XIII as, for example, in the well-known song which Valle wrote before the Republic came into being:

Alfonso, be careful
and take off, for things
in Spain go badly.

Else, the sovereign people
might cut your
head off.

Alfonso, ten pestaña
Y ahueca el ala
que la cosa en España
se pone mala.

No sea que
el pueblo soberano
te dé mulé.

His anticlericalism, so evident throughout his work, but especially in the *esperpentos* and in the *Ruedo ibérico*, was common knowledge to all his friends. The daily *La Voz* picked up the words pronounced by Don Ramón as he lay dying when he answered his friend Andrés Díaz de Rábago's suggestion that he, Don Ramón, should prepare himself to die. Don Ramón wanted "no humble friar, tactful priest, nor know-it-all Jesuit."[5]

It was Antonio Machado, whose opinions Pedro Salinas did not include in the *Indice Literario* article, who most forcefully praised through his character and double, Juan de Mairena, "that profoundly religious aspect of Valle's death":

> . . . the solemn order he gave his family to arrange for him a civil burial. How few expected it! Out there, in admirable Compostela, with its cathedral, its town-hall, and its archbishop—what a magnificent setting for Bradomín's burial! But Valle-Inclán, the inspired creator of Bradomín, respected truth even more than fantasy. His last words, addressed to Death, were full of the impatience of the poet: 'This is taking much too long!' How well Don Ramón handled himself in that supreme moment of adversity, to which Jorge Manrique had alluded![6]

There are several texts of Machado which prove his admiration for Valle-Inclán, some in verse, others in prose. There are two sonnets, one dedicated to *Flor de santidad*, the other written for a celebration honoring Don Ramón, an event Machado was not able to attend. As for the texts in prose, besides the passage from *Juan de Mairena* quoted above, there are the lines from *Los complementarios* in which Machado affirms that "until now no one has written, in Spanish, in a way so perfect and finished as Don Ramón del Valle-Inclán." But even more important are two other texts: the letter he writes to Don Ramón to thank him for sending *La lámpara maravillosa*;[7] and the edition of *La corte de los milagros*. Out of that prologue, less known than it should be, I shall quote only this sentence: "No one carried poverty and the ill fortunes of the Spanish man of letters with more dignity and absence of begging than our Don Ramón del Valle-Inclán." Then Machado adds that, had Valle-Inclán lived in July of 1936,

> he would be with us today, with all of us who sympathize with the people and embrace their cause. It would be difficult, certainly, for him to find a party in which he could be militantly orthodox, or which would coincide exactly with his political ideology. But, in the face of Spain's invasion by foreigners and the treachery from inside Spain itself, there would have been a rebirth in Don Ramón of the leader of noble causes he carried within, and many of his dreamt-of deeds could have become realities.

It is idle to conjecture what might have happened, but given Don Ramón's antimilitarism and anticlericalism it is quite likely that, had he lived in July of 1936 in his native Galicia, he would not have fared well there. In any case he would not have been any better off in Santiago than Unamuno was in Salamanca.

And, since we have mentioned Machado's admiration for Valle-Inclán, it would not be excessive to emphasize his opinion that we "should forget the copious collection of anecdotes about his life" and instead "read and study his books and admire his incomparable pages."

Corpus Barga has evoked a certain evening in January 1939, when Machado, on his way to exile, whiled away his hours in a farmhouse near Gerona remembering Valle-Inclán. Says Barga:

> 'Do you remember,' Machado asked me, 'those nights in the cafés of Madrid? Do you not feel that we have done Valle-Inclán harm, telling so many stories about him? But the fact is, that things did happen to him . . . Do you remember that story of his about disguising himself as a Capuchin monk and which he ended by telling calmly, as if it were the most natural thing in the world, that the other Capuchin, the real one, and himself had returned

> on foot from Valladolid to Madrid in five hours?' One evening I witnessed the telling of the anecdote, and as he finished mentioning the five hours, one of the people who was listening to him from a distance got up and, gesturing farewell, exclaimed: 'A good pace you must have kept, Father Valle!' 'But,' Machado continues, 'we ought not tell the anecdotes of Valle-Inclán, be they the ones he told or those told by others. It is now time for us to study his work and take note of its importance.'[8]

When I read this article by Corpus Barga the story seemed to me familiar. Machado himself tells it in the prologue to *La corte de los milagros,* the edition published in Barcelona. There are two variants in Machado's version: it was not five hours but four that it took Valle to get from Valladolid to Madrid, and he had been disguised not as a Capuchin friar but as a Trappist.

Machado was not alone in calling for the ridding of the anecdotal in Valle-Inclán. Among others, Ramón Sender has expressed the same opinion in his book *Valle-Inclán y la dificultad de la tragedia.*[9] "The best way to do justice to Valle-Inclán," writes Sender, "is to attempt an intelligent criticism of his work and to forget anecdotes which are of little consequence. This is relatively simple because they were the least significant thing about him." But the ridding of the anecdotal material has not been deemed desirable by all critics. Azorín, in the prologue to the complete works of Valle-Inclán (Editorial Plenitud) affirms that he "inevitably needed the anecdote as a way of venting his emotions, in order to recover, in a way, from his intense and exhausting work," adding:

> And this, aside from the fact that an aspect of Valle-Inclán's genius had its complement—however ephemeral those anecdotes gathered by the biographer. One thing could not be given without the other . . . And when we speak of a complement of the inner life with the exterior, we enter fully into the center of Valle-Inclán's self; for

> one of those aspects of Valle-Inclán's personality is the verbal invention of the creator: the verbal imagination unfolded in his innermost being had by force, by necessity, to continue externally. We do not imagine Valle-Inclán's multicolored and pluriformed language to be hidden away, without finding its way into the street, the *tertulia,* and the tumultuous public demonstrations.

Francisco Ayala is even more insistent in defending the importance of anecdotes for the better understanding of Valle-Inclán's personality. Ayala has written:

> Anecdotes and picturesque elements surrounding Valle-Inclán's personality are not merely accessory. Nor should they be looked upon with disdain. On the contrary, they are very important. They are, in short, essential. For, like Quevedo, with whom he has always, and rightly, been compared (and unlike those other creative people who prefer to conceal themselves, to fade out as individuals, such as Galdós), Valle belongs to that kind of personality whose life is an example of involvement and inseparableness from his work.[10]

I am in agreement with both Azorín and Ayala. Many anecdotes are revealing of a character, of a personality, and that personality is inseparable from the writer's destiny—of the writer Valle-Inclán, as well as of the literary history of Spain. Azorín is correct when he writes in the prologue quoted above:

> That moving document will automatically find a place in our literary history: next to Cristóbal de Castillejo's dialogue with his pen, next to Cervantes' painful confession in his *Viaje al Parnaso*; next to the letters of Góngora, no less plain than Valle-Inclán's letter; and finally, next to Moratín's letters from Paris.

One famous sentence of Don Ramón gives us still another example: the one he uttered at the banquet given him by his friends in the Madrid restaurant Fornos in April of 1922. "The curse of Spanish intellectuals is like that of the gypsies: to be persecuted by the Civil Guard."[11] Is this a merely accessory and superficial remark? Not at all. It is rather the testimony of an important intellectual who knew what he was saying; and a declaration that has not lost meaning in our own time. The frustrated homage paid to Antonio Machado in Baeza, in February of 1966, at which several hundreds of Spanish intellectuals were persecuted and beaten by the Civil Guard, will unfortunately not be the last example which will make Don Ramón's sentence a reality. And the reader will remember that the two intellectuals in *Los cuernos de don Friolera,* Don Estrafalario and Don Manolito, who reappear at the end of the play, find themselves in prison, accused of being anarchists and of having cast an evil eye on a jackass.

Moreover, it is well known that Valle himself thought highly of his anecdotes and considered them an integral part of his personality. When he wrote his last will and testament in verse he did not forget them. It is certainly worth reading, but not in the version given by Gómez de la Serna in his book on Valle; rather it should be read in another, less known, published by Camilo José Cela,[12] which doubtless is an improvement on the previous one. Here is the text:

> I leave my dead body to you, newshound.
> The day they take me to be buried cold,
> you'll smoke at my expense a good cigar,
> and at "la Rumba" your stomach you will stuff.
>
> And after dining on my poor remains,
> pickled in your familiar subtle style,
> the stogie smoking and your hunger past,
> you will abuse me with your wit so vile.
>
> And as you leave the butt inside the wine glass,
> still half-full upon the tablecloth,

you will say, as you take your bicarbonate,
"I hope Don Miguel doesn't kick it yet!"

To you, newshound, I bequeath my body.
And my anecdotes, they are all for you!
Out of my funeral you'll get more money
than in my mortal life I ever knew.

So, gentlemen, good health and better luck.
My lamp now falters and will soon go out.
The hand of death has hung a warning sign
around the ivory tower where I live.

To the owner of the corner tavern
I leave my laurels to adorn his door;
my palm leaves, to a lady's balcony,
and all the tinsel to a raving mask.

Te dejo mi cadáver, reportero.
El día que me lleven a enterrar
fumarás a mi costa un buen veguero,
te darás en "La Rumba" un buen yantar,

Y después de cenar con mi fiambre,
abodabo en retórica sutil,
humeando el puro, satisfecha el hambre,
me injuriará tu dicharacho vil.

Y al dejar la colilla con el chato
a medio consumir, sobre el mantel,
dirás gustando del bicarbonato,
"¡Que no la diñe ahora don Miguel!"

Para ti mi cadáver, reportero,
mis anécdotas, ¡todas para ti!
Le sacas a mi entierro más dinero
que en mi vida mortal yo nunca vi.

Caballeros, salud y buena suerte.
Da sus últimas luces mi candil.
Ha colgado la mano de la muerte
papeles en mi torre de marfil.

Le dejo al tabernero de la esquina,
para adornar su puerta, mi laurel.
Mis palmas, al balcón de una vecina,
y a una máscara loca, el oropel.

Valle-Inclán thought, no doubt, as Miguel de Unamuno, who used to say, "If they deprive us of legend, what have we left?"[13]

Now leaving aside this aspect of Don Ramón's personality, let us ask ourselves: what is Valle-Inclán's posthumous fortune in Spain? That fortune is curious indeed, especially in relation to his dramatic works. The history of Valle-Inclán's drama oscillates between oblivion and ecclesiastical ban, on the one hand (it was proscribed during the first years following the war), and on the other, the recent performances in Madrid of *Divinas palabras* and *Águila de blasón*, and the enthusiastic adherence of the new generation critical of this second work.

The hundred articles published in the Madrid press when Valle-Inclán died cannot hide a shameful fact: the scarce critical interest in his work. Pedro Salinas was the first one to point this out. "Valle-Inclán's work," he writes, "has not yet received the thorough study it deserves." I repeated the same complaint eleven years later, in 1947.[14] Why was there such a lack of critical interest? Was it because critics were afraid to face a labor so full of difficulties, as Ramón Sender believes?[15] Or was it because it was feared that the ideological roots which would explain Valle-Inclán's evolution would have to be admitted?[16] Possibly both. But it was also inevitable that Valle-Inclán's work should suffer the oscillations of literary taste, as well as the low esteem the baroque has suffered during the last thirty or forty years. In 1958 I ventured to prophesy: "It is quite likely that there will be a return to Valle-Inclán not many years from now, just as there is now taking place a return to Galdós."[17] When I wrote those lines there was absolute silence regarding Valle-Inclán's works, especially his drama. But it was not difficult to predict the change, for by then one began to feel a certain boredom with realism in literature. There was a new interest in the imaginative, an eminent example of which is Valle-Inclán's creativity. Can it be affirmed that my prophecy has been fulfilled, and that it is possible to speak today of a return to Valle-Inclán? It seems evident to me that this is the case. As proof of this we have the numerous activities occasioned by the centenary of his birth. Pedro Salinas' complaint in January of 1936 would not be justified today, given the many studies on Valle-Inclán published during the last thirty years. The bibliography on his work has been enriched considerably in the last six years, and Antonio Odriozola, in the bibliographical count he published in the *Insula*[18] issue dedicated to Valle-Inclán, estimates that the number of articles that could be gathered in a new bibliography goes beyond seven hundred.

Coming back to Valle-Inclán's dramatic works, it seems to me useful to recall the old argument as to whether or not they are fit for the stage; whether they can be performed and a public found for them. Those who believe that Valle-Inclán's drama is not for the stage usually point out the difficulties Don Ramón himself met with in staging some of his works for the first time. They like to remember his bitter complaints. In a letter dated November 12, 1913, Valle-Inclán wrote to a friend:

> Dear Barinaga: I have received *Romance de lobos*. Don't forget to send me the rest of the papers. And now something else. If you notice that it is difficult for Fuentes [the actor Francisco Fuentes] to stage my works, tell him that he is under no obligation to me, and that the fact he does not perform them cannot offend me, for no one better than I knows they are not works for the public, especially a provincial public. They are works fit for a one-night stand in Madrid, and that's all. I don't say this out of modesty. On the contrary. Our day will come; but for the moment it is not yet in sight. I should feel bad if Fuentes, through lack of frankness with me, and his fear of displeasing me,

> would want to hide this fact, a fact I know so well. I am now engaged in a new play, and if it has an easier time reaching the public, as is my hope, I will send it to him. And so tell him not to spend anything on those works. Whatever new I write, having acquired more skill, will be more viable. And especially since I will employ all my efforts to make it so, for we must make a lot of money, my dear Barinaga. Many regards to Paco, and to you an affectionate embrace from your old friend Valle Inclán.[19]

This letter points out three things. First, that in 1913,—the year he published *La marquesa Rosalinda* and *El embrujado,* which had been refused for the stage by Galdós, then artistic director of the Teatro Español in Madrid (a reading in the Ateneo of the same play did not have any effect either)—Valle-Inclán continued to write hoping to make his début and "a lot of money." Second, that in spite of it, Don Ramón knew that his works did not please the public, and that at best they were fit for a "one-night stand." And third, that he nevertheless expected to see the day, which "for the moment is not in sight," when his own drama would take hold. Valle-Inclán, then, had faith in his drama. The enthusiasm of young Spanish critics is proof that Valle-Inclán was right. As we shall see presently, young critics have for some years been pressing for the performance of Valle-Inclán's dramatic works in the theatres of Madrid, thus creating a favorable mood which has at least permitted the performance of two of his plays, *Divinas palabras* and *Águila de blasón*, the former with considerable success.

Other critics have denied that there is viability in the dramatic works of Valle-Inclán, and such had been the opinion of Pedro Salinas.[20] Ramón Sender, in his *Valle-Inclán y la dificultad de la tragedia* has written:

> *Divinas palabras* is not a work meant for the stage, and could not please the public . . . The truth is that Don

> Ramón's are not really plays. They abound in lyric density but are lacking in plasticity, psychological movement, and that interplay of contrary realities between the stage and the drawing room without which only one kind of drama has been possible: classical tragedy.

Who could tolerate, asked Sender, Valle-Inclán's bold realism on the stage? And Sender ends his argument affirming that Valle-Inclán's drama, with its mixture of farce and tragedy, is as impossible to perform as *La Celestina.* But these arguments are not acceptable if applied to our own time. What Sender calls the "bold realism" of Valle-Inclán, such as the mixture of farce and tragedy, is today very much in line with the most contemporary theatre, which fears nothing. After the success of *Divinas palabras* one can no longer insist that the plays of Valle-Inclán are not fit for the stage. Just as Unamuno was a precursor of Existentialism, so is Valle-Inclán a precursor of the so-called theatre of the absurd. Spanish criticism has pointed out the modernity of his dramaturgy, how it anticipates the neo-expressionistic theatre of today with its mixture of the farcical and tragic, and the technique of the *esperpento.* Ricardo Domenech has seen in Valle-Inclán's *esperpentos,* with their dislocation of reality, something silimar to what Bertolt Brecht intended with his technique of detachment, in which the spectator does not become nullified, absorbed in the emotion of the play, but rather becomes conscious of reality, both of his reality and that of the society which surrounds him.[21]

However, to affirm Valle-Inclán's modernity is not to deny the difficulties his dramaturgy has presented and indeed continues to present in order to reach a normal status in the Spanish theatre such as that enjoyed by García Lorca, to cite only one example. Such difficulties have been enormous and continue to exist, although to a lesser extent. I shall allude to them briefly. But in order to do so I shall have to go back and refer to the situation of the Spanish theatre during the years immediately following the Civil War. If Valle-Inclán's plays were already ignored by theatrical managers before the war, in post-war Spain they were to be banned. Everything conspired against Valle-Inclán. It was not only the memory of a leftist and anti-clerical Valle-Inclán, a friend of the Soviet Union, but his drama itself, which is difficult, sarcastic, and corrosive. As with everyone of the Generation of 1898, with the exception of Maeztu and Azorín, Valle-Inclán's writings were forbidden. Censorship had complete control over all phases of art; and if we remember what Spanish culture was like in those years, we should have to admit that the panorama was much gloomier than what it was when Rubén Darío made his second trip to Spain in 1898. With Valle-Inclán, Unamuno, Machado and Lorca dead, and Juan Ramón Jiménez, Ortega and the majority of the poets and writers of the Generation of 1927 in exile, the Spanish cultural scene could not have been more barren. As for the theatre, with Casona and Jacinto Grau in exile, and with Valle-Inclán, Unamuno, and Lorca banned, it could literally be said not to exist. When the editor Ruiz Castillo decided in 1944 to publish Valle-Inclán's complete works in two volumes, with prologues by Azorín and Benavente, an official review, *La Estafeta Literaria,* initiated an inquiry about Valle-Inclán.[22] It was the first time that a review held a debate about Valle-Inclán and his work in post-war Spain. To the question whether Valle-Inclán's drama remained alive in its time the answers were affirmative. José Vicente Puente laments, nevertheless—and it is the first time that a complaint is heard publicly—the shameful fact that no attempt was made to perform any of the brilliant poet's masterpieces. And he adds: "I have looked for Valle-Inclán's name everywhere: in the programs of legitimate theatres; and in declarations made by theatrical managers. It is as if he had been forgotten, as if he never existed. Our own generation scarcely knows him." A dramatist of the time, Victor Ruiz Iriarte, exclaimed: "Why, of course, Valle-Inclán's dramatic works remain through the years, proud and fascinating!" Ten years later, in another review, Luis Trabozo wrote:

> Today's fashions are not propitious to Valle-Inclán. The younger generation neither likes nor esteems him. Nor, I think, does it understand him fully. He is taken to be, first of all, a delicate writer. And that is why he is considered *démodé* . . . It is quite possible that in these statements Baroja, whose opinions are, to my way of thinking, unjust and superficial, may be influential.[23]

Ten years later the scene had changed. As we shall presently see, Spanish intellectual youth will demonstrate wide enthusiasm for the work of Valle-Inclán.

During those years there appeared some studies on Valle-Inclán: in 1943, the biography by Fernández Almagro; in 1944, that of Ramón Gómez de la Serna, widely distributed in the Austral edition; in 1945, Laín's book on the Generation of 1898; and in 1946 the review *Cuadernos de Literatura Contemporánea* dedicated an issue to Valle-Inclán, the first one to pay him homage in post-war Spain. The following years saw the appearance of works by Zamora Vicente, Augustín del Saz, Pérez Minik, etc. And in 1961 the review *Insula* dedicated a number to him. The tone in the latter was strongly favorable. The movement towards a climate of enthusiasm for and a return to Valle-Inclán had begun. But his plays continued to be scandalously absent from the Spanish stage. Since the end of the Spanish Civil War, eighteen years had to go by before even an attempt was made to produce one of his plays. This was *La marquesa Rosalinda*, perhaps because its eighteenth century and Modernist air seemed more innocuous to those who arranged its performance. It took place in March, 1957, at the Reina Victoria theatre, in Madrid, pompously called Teatro Popular del Departamento de Cultura de la Delegación de Educación Popular. It was a drawing room theatre, and the only performance went by practically unnoticed. However, mention should be made of an excellent article by

Melchor Fernández Almagro, explaining that first revival of a play by Valle-Inclán in the theatres of Madrid.[24] In 1959, the Teatro Universitario, directed by Juan José Alonso revived, though also for one single performance, *Los cuernos de don Friolera.* But even the title appeared too bold to those responsible for culture in the Madrid of the period. The play was billed with the title *Don Friolera*, prudishly depriving it of the horns. The performance was a success but it had little repercussion. The same was not true when this group put on the play in the Teatro Romea of Murcia, again with the title *Don Friolera.* There were protests, and one spectator, a former soldier in Franco's army, exclaimed indignantly "and for this we won the war!" The Murcia press took the side of the protester. The newspaper *La Verdad* published a violent article titled "Protestamos," saying, among other things:

> Yesterday we protested energetically in our theatre section the shame to which our city has been subjected in the midst of traditional celebrations, by some groups of Teatro Universitario students, though Spaniards, who came to perform some plays in every way repulsive, and who have offered one of the most lamentable spectacles we have seen in several years. These *esperpentos* should not have been performed, neither for the sake of the works selected, nor for those who selected them, nor yet again for the sake of the public to which the play was destined, and which deserved greater respect. It is a great pity that we should have to say this twenty years after the profound change in Spain! This change which Don Ramón del Valle-Inclán and company tried so hard to prevent! We do not believe that anyone can accuse us of being against the avant-garde, or anything like it. But since when have the avant-garde, progress, and the advancement of humanity been realized while leaning on vice? Must we revive Valle-Inclán for the sake of the avant-garde? And especially this Valle-Inclán? Can we

> permit the return of a period, of a political situation, and of men so savagely destructive? Can we allow the return of insults to institutions so fundamental as the Army? What our Spain of today needs is certainly not the politics of Valle-Inclán's Spain.[25]

But such protests could not prevent the inevitable. The movement to restore Valle-Inclán to his rightful place was given impetus by the best of Spain's youth, especially by young university students. It was the generation of 1950 that raised the battle cry in favor of Valle-Inclán's drama, striving to renew the best of the literary tradition. In 1960, a writer of the generation of 1950, Alfredo Mañas, published an article on Valle-Inclán in the review of the Facultad de Filosofía y Letras de Madrid,[26] in which he defended Valle-Inclán's return to the Spanish stage. Wrote Mañas:

> Why have Valle-Inclán's dramatic works not been staged in Spain when there have been revived so many other plays inferior to his? Assuredly because someone has let the rumor run that his plays were not for the public, that they were not what is recognized as good theatre. Or because another has asked smugly how one can present a boat on the stage. Because some hypocrite dressed in peasant's clothes has said Valle-Inclán is sensual and violent. Who knows? Any excuse will do to exclude anyone who does not please us. Any pretext will do to exile a man from his country's theatre, even when, as Azorín says, this man has given his country's literature a real treasure. Any pretext will do to convert a man, who ought to continue being the central axis of the National Theatre, into a forgotten classic. Such a man is Valle-Inclán: father of Spain's contemporary theatre.

It is clear that the dramatist Alfredo Mañas is thinking of Federico García Lorca and of himself, whose play *La feria de cuernicabra,* successfully performed in Madrid, owes much to Don Ramón's dramaturgy.

That same generation of 1950 fights in favor of Valle-Inclán's dramas, in open discussion, on the stage, and in literary reviews. By 1961 the generation of 1950 reaches maturity and its fight in favor of Valle-Inclán's theatre gives its first results. *Divinas palabras* is staged successfully in the Bellas Artes Theatre of Madrid; the Grupo de Teatro Realista, directed by Alfonso Sastre and José María de Quinto, launches a manifesto asking that homages be paid to Valle-Inclán; and two reviews of prestige *Insula* and *Primer Acto,* dedicate several numbers to his honor.[27] Who remembers now the anger shown by the little Murcia newspaper? In *Primer Acto* the young writers of the generation of 1950—Alfonso Sastre, José Monleón, José María de Quinto, and Ricardo Domenech affirmed their adherence to and enthusiasm for Valle-Inclán. Thus they joined hands with the war generation critics Gonzalo Torrente Ballester, Adolfo Prego, and Fernando Baeza. In that magazine, José Monleón, the director, wrote: "Valle is probably the author most admired by the Spanish younger generation.. His influence is being felt more and more. Valle the 'aesthete' is quite frankly the dramatist most *engagé* with the total reality of Spain. And yet," he adds, "*Luces de Bohemia,* one of the great masterpieces of the Spanish genius, of non-conformity and black humor, has not premiered." As for *Insula,* writers of four generations came together in response to a poll I myself prepared concerning the dramatic works of Valle-Inclán. There was the Generation of 1898 represented by Azorín; that of Ortega represented by Pérez de Ayala; the generation of 1927 by Claudio de la Torre and by the critic Sergio Nerva (Antonio Rodríguez de León); and the post-war generation, represented by Antonio Buero Vallejo, Fernando Lázaro, Alfonso Sastre, Pablo Martí Zaro and Francisco Sitjá. All claim for Valle-Inclán what he justly deserves: the rank of a great creator of dramatic art, with every right to a place in the

Spanish theatre. I shall single out two of these responses. Buero Vallejo wrote:

> When we read *La hija del capitán* and other works by Valle-Inclán, we are filled with wonder. They almost appear to have been written in our own day by some dramatic commentator who knows our deepest wounds. A marginal writer for the stage in his own day, he was and is a great dramatist, formidably revealing his country and the gloomy and obvious sides of human truth. Ignorance of Valle-Inclán's theatre is due not so much to circumstance as to willfulness. It is the result of the tenacious hostility of those who prefer death to life, and mediocrity to talent. His absence from our stage is due more to a diffuse conspiracy than to a spontaneous phenomenon.

For his part, Alfonso Sastre affirms:

> Valle-Inclán is one of the great masters of European theatre in our times . . . We must claim for him his place as a master, notwithstanding the purely circumstantial fact that he has or has not disciples or followers, whether or not he is well known in Europe. If he is not now well known, he will surely be in due time. His dramaturgy means the autonomous Spanish discovery of dramatic expressionism, the anticipation of the anti-psychological element in the later social drama, and the deliberate use of "distancing" which Brecht would later employ.

And now we come to 1966, the year of Valle-Inclán's centennial. Officially, as concerns Spain, it has been a poor centennial in every sense, without ambition or quality. Only one play of Don Ramón's has been staged (in the María Guerrero theatre.) But that play, *Águila de blasón*, dates from 1907. This means that it belongs to Valle-Inclán's early period, characteristically Modernist, esthetically speaking, and is not what we should have liked to see performed. It would have been more worthy to stage one of the cutting and rending *esperpentos, Luces de Bohemia, Los cuernos de don Friolera* or *La hija del capitán*, for example. To make matters even worse, the version given of *Águila de blasón* was one mutilated by censorship, the language combed and toned down. Official Spain, it seems, still fears Valle-Inclán. There is a fear, especially, of confronting the popular public with Valle-Inclán's more lively and modern drama, best represented by the *esperpentos*. (The bourgeois, snobbish public is not dangerous: everything skips it without as much as touching its conscience.) Those who believe there is an art and a culture whose influence is dangerous for the people, and must therefore remain buried, fear above all the public's awareness. *Águila de blasón* did not post such a danger, and was for that reason chosen to commemorate its author's centenary. And it naturally did not merit the brash remarks made by the daily *ABC's* drama critic as he commented on the performance: "Valle's drama is dead, dead, dead!" To that we can only answer, parodying Don Juan, that the dead whom they attempt to kill continue to enjoy good health.

NOTES

[1] An account of the Teatro de la Zarzuela event can be read in the newspaper *El Sol*, February 5, 1936.

[2] Number 1 for 1936. Salinas included it in his book *Literatura española Siglo XX*, México, Antigua Librería Robredo, 1949, (Second Edition).

[3] *La Voz*, January 6, 1936.

[4] *Ibid.*

[5] *Ibid.* Domingo García-Sabell, a friend of Don Ramón's was frequently with him the last few months, and knew well his radical political and anticlerical views. See my essay in *Revista de Occidente*, December, 1966.

[6] *El Sol*. January 19, 1936. Compiled in *Juan de Mairena.*

[7] Can be read today in: Antonio Machado, *Obras*, Losada. 1966, edited by Guillermo de Torre and Aurora de Albornoz.

[8] *La Estafeta literaria*, No. 343, May, 1966.

[9] Editorial Gredos, Madrid, 1965.

[10] *Insula*, Nos. 236–237, July–August, 1966.

[11] The daily *La Voz* on January 6, 1936, gave the following version: "The

ideal of Spanish intellectuals should be the life of the gypsy, who lives always outside the law and is forever persecuted by the police.

[12] Camilo José Cela, "Las memorias de Baroja y la última cuartilla de Valle-Inclán." In Clavileño, No. 2, March–April, 1950. Two versions have been given regarding the poem's origin. According to Ramón Gómez de la Serna it is a reply to a question asked by an insolent newspaperman, who asked stupidly: "¿Cuándo la diñamos, Don Ramón? [When do we kick the bucket, Don Ramón?]" *Indice de Artes y Letras* in its number dedicated to Valle-Inclán (74–75, 1954) gives a different version. In an anonymous note it says, "In October of 1932, Valle-Inclán became so gravely ill that a newspaperman offered the doorkeeper of the house in which he lived five *duros* if she would give him before anyone else notice of his death." Don Ramón found out and wrote the *Testamento* poem. The *Indice* version, which includes a reproduction of the *Testamento* in the writer's own hand, although not complete, contradicts Cela's affirmation that Valle-Inclán wrote the poem only a few days before he died. Although the reproduction in *Indice* follows in the beginning Cela's version, the end contains some lines of the version published by Gómez de la Serna. It is probable, then, that Valle-Inclán made several corrections. The original version would be that published by Gómez de la Serna, who says it was Don Ramón's sons who gave it to him; an intermediate text would be the incomplete one reproduced by *Indice*—and the only one in the writer's hand I know; and the final version the one published by Cela, without mention of the source.

[13] See "Carta" to Dámaso Alonso, in *Pensamiento y letras en la España del Siglo XX.* Vanderbilt University, 1966, p. 7.

[14] *Insula,* No. 22, October, 1947.

[15] Ramón J. Sender, *Valle-Inclán y la dificultad de la tragedia.* Madrid, Gredos, 1965, p. 8.

[16] José María de Quinto, "Un teatro desconocido: el de Valle-Inclán." *Insula,* July–August, 1966.

[17] "Retorno de Valle-Inclán," *Insula,* no. 140, 1958.

[18] *Insula,* Nos. 236–237, July–August, 1966.

[19] *Primer Acto,* November, 1961.

[20] "Neither the Comedias Bárbaras nor the rest of Valle-Inclán's dramatic works are meant to be performed. They are meant to be read . . ." Pedro Salinas, *Literatura española siglo XX,* México, 1949, pp. 92–93.

[21] Lecture given in the Asociación Española de Mujeres Universitarias de Madrid.

[22] No. 1, January, 1945.

[23] "El mundo poético de Valle-Inclán." In *Indice de Artes y Letras.* No. 74–75, 1954.

[24] *ABC,* Madrid, March 21, 1957.

[25] April 8, 1959.

[26] Alfredo Mañas, "Don Ramón del Valle-Inclán," *Cuadernos de Arte y Pensamiento,* No. 4, Nov. 1960, pp. 150–154.

[27] *Primer Acto,* No. 28, Nov., 1961; *Insula,* No. 176–177, July–August, 1961.

RICARDO GULLÓN

REALITY OF THE *ESPERPENTO*

Translated by

MIGUEL GONZÁLEZ-GERTH

I

The *esperpento,* certainly, has the unreal reality of art. But if we speak of reality in more inclusive terms, we may say that the *esperpento* reveals it. Contrary to common opinion, the *esperpento*, either as Valle-Inclán or as others conceived it, was used to approach reality in a more lucid and open-eyed way than the so-called realistic way. The idea was to discover what we might call the "essence" of reality. If I hesitate to use this term it is because I am not sure that one may speak of such an "essence," since by its very nature the reality to which I am referring—that which interests the novelist—is a reality subject to time and space; it is an ever-changing historical reality.

In Valle-Inclán's case, it was perhaps his awareness of this historical reality, present in him since the twenties, which turned him toward the *esperpento*. (To be sure, certain elements and tendencies suggesting this technique are rather frequent in his early work, but what was then merely occasional and diffuse was later to become constant and coherent.)

Luces de Bohemia contains the reality of the world Valle-Inclán inhabits, not the reality of a world he imagines, as was the case with *La guerra carlista.* Bradomín, Montenegro, and Cara de Plata belong to a world where heroism could seem possible (at least to them), a world with feudal overtones, recreated freely by the author's imagination since he had never really known it. Max Estrella and Captain Chuletas de Sargento are farcial "heroes" because like their creator, they live in a society where the individual—and consequently heroic acts—have lost their meaning.

As soon as we approach the *esperpento* we notice that its most obvious feature is its mechanization of character. The most affected and miserable are described variously, with a wealth of words, yet they are always defined by terms which express the same thing: mechanization; marionettes, puppets, automats, dummies, dolls—they are called, and that is how they behave. They react when their strings are tugged. Their expressions are exaggerated, jerky movements; their gestures, scrawls; and their postures are controlled by a clever puppeteer who knows his business well. The mechanical effect is unintentional. It recalls the process by which man, in modern society, becomes a mere thing. For the individual continually loses significance as he is dealt with more and more cynically, as a tiny piece of the collective mass to which he must subordinate himself. The very concept of the hero demands an autonomous behavior that contemporary society seldom allows for.

Marxists (and non-Marxists) hold that a gradual curtailment of freedom comes from exchanging a liberal economy for an imperialistic capitalism. This is a problem which cannot be discussed within the limits of this essay; I will state that in such a genuine process of dehumanization (from which was derived, for two equally spontaneous reasons—one of moral protest, the other of artistic loyalty to a deeper reality—the misnamed "dehumanization of art") is the key to Valle-Inclán's aesthetic. So it is not surprising that Valle-Inclán's change of perspective was accompanied—or preceded—by his adoption of a political and social radicalism manifested in extremist attitudes. He enthusiastically supported the social aspect of the Mexican Revolution (*"y lo primero / ahorcar al encomendero"*) ("and the first thing / is to hang the *encomendero*") and joined the *Congreso de defensa de la Cultura,* as well as the organization known as *Amigos de la Unión Soviética,* although he admired certain accomplishments of Italian fascism. Such attitudes seem to me to stem from Valle-Inclán's belief that the most urgent need at the time was to stave off the materialism of a society ruled by the idea of profit.

Valle-Inclán's aesthetic nostalgia for archaic ways of life revealed in his early works joins with his later expressed hope for futuristic ways of life. And both—the nostalgia and the hope—have in common a harmony in the human relations typical during his time and ours: that these relations will remain human as long as the idea of profit does not turn men into things by using them as a ready means to the ultimate end which, from Guizot (*"enrichessez-vous!"*) to McMillan ("you've never had it so good"), has so often been proclaimed by realistic politicians.

The man who has become a "thing" is like any other object in the world. It is not surprising that, in order to emphasize this likeness, Valle-Inclán should turn the technique around, describing an inanimate object—a piano, a toy car—as if it were animate. In *La corte de los milagros*, Adolfito Bonifaz and his friend toss a policeman out of a window, killing him. They think the act is insignificant, because in their minds the guard is not a human being but merely a handy thing for their entertainment. And naturally the act does more than turn the victim into a thing; it dehumanizes the spoiled boys, emphasizes their inhumanity. A man cannot remain human if he denies the humanity of other men. Tirano Banderas, isolated in his tower of cruelty and silence, turns everyone around him into an animal or even a machine. But, by the same token, he cannot remain human himself, since he must share the animality and mechanization he imposes on his victims.

In *Tirano Banderas* the Spanish pawnbroker, Quintín Pereda, is not exempt from automatism because of his wealth, nor does power save General Narváez from having an animal nature. In using the *esperpento,* Valle-Inclán presents his imaginative vision of an ontological crisis directly related to a social phenomenon: the negation of the individual's freedom and even the individual himself. When this happens, there can be no genuine human behavior. The tough Narváez and the usurious Pereda can no more escape the mechanism of which they are part than the policeman murdered by Bonifaz and his cronies, or the little Indian woman victimized by the same Pereda. On the other hand, once a certain level of suffering has been reached, a victim of circumstances, a victim whose part in such circumstances is passive and accidental, can be humanized again. This is the case of Zacarías. When he discovers the remains of his child half-devoured by the hogs, he is turned to stone by his silent, paralyzing grief which, in its sheer intensity, frees him from his social conditioning and allows him—unknowingly—to regain his freedom as a man.

If the *esperpento* is a vehicle for this type of intuition, then its negation of so-called realism (as a novelistic technique) represents an oblique means of restoring reality. It destroys our faith in ideas, values and methods by forcing us to face an ambiguity that makes us feel insecure. In his *Sonatas*, Valle-Inclán offered us a lie in disguise, fiction as imagination, romance as it might naturally be idealized. But from *Luces de Bohemia* on, he strives to present bare truth so as to show that the reality of the realists is unacceptable, whereas the *esperpentesque* caricature is a much less tricky approximation because it does not attempt to deceive the eye as the former method does. Actually, the break with realism had already taken place in the idealizing tendency of his early period, which gave rise to as much distortion and more improbability than his later tendency did. What happened was that in the later works, the reader was more easily able to recognize fragments of everyday life. Instead of concealing anything, the deforming distortion actually emphasized the breakdown of traditional values. Referring to the modern world, Gottfried Benn once warned: "Reality no longer exists; only its caricature does."[1]

That caricature was to be the starting point for a reconstruction of a reality which, to be sure, would never again seem as solid as it had in the past. Ever since the *esperpento*, there has been a suspicion that reality may not be as real as our ancestors thought. The destructive effect of these works is exactly what was needed to reveal what lies under the make-up; how to find the depths of a reality which has been adulterated, buried under a beguiling superstructure. This revelatory intention necessarily submitted the subject matter to a degrading treatment. A myth cannot be destroyed unless the person who embodies it is belittled, brought down to a lower level—degraded.

The effects of Valle-Inclán's demythicizing technique in his *esperpentos* are swift and devastating. One example will suffice: "Robust and seductive, her Catholic Majesty [Isabella II] smiled in the manner of the woman who sells doughnuts in the church of the Virgen de la Paloma." What the author does, obviously, is condense in a short sentence two antithetical terms, producing a kind of oxymoron which emphasizes a manifold being and its natural contradictions while, at the same time, abolishing the myth of a "Divine, Catholic, Royal Majesty." Valle presents a grotesque husband even more concisely: "King Francis whined like a lap dog beside the queen's bodily opulence." The monarch—albeit only a royal consort in this instance—is reduced to the state of a snivelling puppy.

Now we can appreciate how accurate Valle was in considering Goya the creator of the *esperpento.* One does not need to point to the *Caprichos,* since in "La familia de Carlos IV" we find not merely suggested but actually depicted the contrasts between being and seeming-to-be which Valle would develop with his pen, lingering at times, as if wishing to prolong the reader's expectancy. Consider the following example, already used in another context by Guillermo Díaz-Plaja:[2] "His Excellency Don Jerónimo Fernando Baltasar de Cisneros y Carvajal, Maldonado y Pacheco, Grandee of Spain, Marquis of Torre Mellada, Count of Cetina and Villar del Monte, Cavalier of Seville, Knight of the Order of Alcántara, Recipient of the Grand Cross of the Most Worthy Order of Charles III was a little old blondish man, made-up and perfumed, exhibiting the flightiness of a foolish nun." The longer the series of titles, the more decisive the demythicizing effect. The man of great stature, the illustrious aristocrat, the highly respected gentleman, is utterly destroyed.

Thus one suddenly arrives at "the truth." The same happens through the use of a metaphor or a simple adjective, such as *calavera* (skull), *momia* (mummy), *rata fisgona* (snoopy rat), which define the image of Tirano Banderas. Someone might wonder if this refers to absolute truth. But the fact is that I do not know what "absolute truth" means and wonder if anyone can say there is such a thing. For the truth is not that Queen Isabella is a common woman, that King Francis is a lap dog, or that the Marquis is a sissy. The truth is that although the Queen is a sexy wench, the King an impotent man, and the Marquis an effeminate cuckold, they are also what their titles indicate. They are the one and the other, both; not the simplification and schematization required by either myth or countermyth, both of which are equally conformist and indiscriminate. The "truth" offered by the *esperpento* is equivocal in its substance, as life is; both consist of a contradiction between the elements of being and the elements of seeming-to-be. If the *esperpento* is subversive, it is because it degrades myth, the idea of myth and its value or values, upon which the continuity of the bourgeois world, our world, depends.

II

The concept of character as a multiple being is basic to the creation of the *esperpento*. The demythicizing intent imposes one condition: not to take off the mask (which is impossible, since it sticks to the skin) but to show that the face itself is a mask and that whoever wears one plays a part for which he is sometimes prepared and sometimes not. In successive scenes, a character might appear wearing different masks, or not wearing one at all; but the result is that the reader or spectator cannot help wondering if the "definitive" face, more deceptive because of its naked appearance, is not just as superimposed or false.

My earlier remarks on the reduction of characters to automatons are confirmed by the titles of Valle's works (*Farsa de la enamorada del Rey, Farsa y licencia de la reina castiza, Retablo de la avaricia, la lujuria y la muerte*) as well as by their generic definition: "plays for silhouettes", "melodramas for puppets". At the beginning of each work there is an indication of its meaning. The characters are presented as playing a part and being conscious of it. So many examples could be given and have been given by other critics that it would be superfluous to mention them here. I shall therefore limit myself to the scenes of the "revolutionary" meeting in *Tirano Banderas* and those in *La corte de los milagros,* in the evanescent Marquise's drawing-room. The Prime Minister González Bravo is seen as a bad actor, and Gonzalón Torre-Mellada chases and pummels the majordomo (to get some money from him) as if he were perfunctorily playing a tedious role in a scene he had performed a hundred times.

The awareness of playing a part in life which is not only fictitious but too well-known does not prevent a character from identifying with the part and living it as he is playing it. In *Los cuernos de don Friolera,* this kind of identification is achieved in a zig-zag manner, with the protagonist experiencing vacillations and oscillations; he would gladly be deceived into thinking himself a victim; but finally he must accept, though unwillingly, the role of defender or restorer of his own honor. Upon grasping such acceptance as something imposed from without and corresponding to an idea—or an image—wrought by social convention, the reader or spectator quickly draws a general rule from this particular case. The archetype of the "Calderonian" husband, a physician of his own honor, is fictitious at first and then becomes a reality under the pressure exerted by the concept of honor dictated by social custom and literary tradition.

In the same work, the reader may notice that the person-mask-character chain is not always the result of violence or social conditioning. It stems rather from the possible transformation of an actual prosaic being into an ideal one. When the individual becomes aware of such a possibility, the prestige of the role suddenly offered him is overwhelming and, together with other more worldly stimuli, it makes him behave as would the archetype. The aura surrounding the part arouses in him the wish to play it, as is the case with Doña Loreta and Pachequín, whose mutual attraction is reinforced when they imagine themselves as heavenly beings or, at least, dramatic personages of great renown. Play-acting becomes living when the puppets realize that their roles enable them to participate somehow in the prestige of the archetypes in whose orbit they move. The comic effect is due to the contrast between how they see themselves and what they are, between appearance and ambition. In view of the circumstances, the picture must seem grotesque to the spectator.

It might seem that no drama is really possible at the level of farce, but this is not so. Friolera kills his innocent daughter—not his adulterous wife. The tragic fate does not affect the legend in the least: the popular ballad at the end of this *esperpento* is structurally significant in the comprehension of the work as a whole, for it relates the events as they should have taken place and not as they actually did take place—by accident. Myth is maintained despite reality, and the pictorial weeklies serve—and how effectively!—a function once reserved for bards.

Valle-Inclán could have pronounced the words Ibsen assigned to Julian the Apostate, in *Emperor and Galilean*: "Ancient beauty is no longer beautiful and new truths are no longer true." The *esperpento* transforms both a smile and a painful expression into grimaces, and the question of truth remains only half-answered because, if the negative element—a lie—is evident, the positive is simply inapprehensible.

Now and then buffoonery comes to a halt, and in the sudden stillness of the moment, brought about by the intrusion of something unexpected and tragic (for example, in *Luces de Bohemia,* the murder of the revolutionary worker by the police), there is a change of atmosphere. And the reader, like the characters in the story, suddenly discovers he is in the presence of true drama. The puppets take on a human aspect when they learn that the absurd wandering through the streets at night is something which they share with archetypes; it is the natural way to live or act out the adventure to which poets are destined. On a symbolic level, *Luces de Bohemia* may be considered a descent into Hell which, despite the esperpentesque degradation, retains a pathetic magnificence.

In a sense it is also an exception to the rule. The degrading element, part and parcel of the genre, is not operative when Max Estrella's misadventures are seen at a deeper level. On the contrary: the myth of the poet descending into the darkness in search of truth is more pathetic when (as is the case here) he cannot return to the land of the living. As the end approaches, the darkness surrounding the blind poet gradually brings together the diverse tragicomic or simply grotesque elements. It may be that these, separately, add a touch of degradation to the situation. But the final result, achieved after scenes of sheer drama, in which all buffoonery is gone, is anything but predictable. The myth is not ultimately degraded; it is restored to the world of human values through parable.

Which is why I speak of an exception: the usually demythicizing *esperpento* does not function typically in this case. Instead, through unexpected and sordid ways, it rehabilitates the character of the nocturnal wanderer, Max Estrella. That the circles of Hell should have more to do with taverns than with Dante's vision is perfectly natural. How else could it be, given the Madrilenian setting? The only credible Francesca in Pica Lagartos' tavern is Enriqueta la Pisa-Bien, and the allusions to contemporary political figures are the aesthetic equivalents of Dante's condemnations. The fate of a poet (forgive me for sounding like the chairman of a poetic competition) and that of a mere man are no less tragic for this reason. Maybe moreso, because the baseness of the environment and of those who inhabit it takes away the greatness of the protagonist's journey to the lower depths. Dante had Virgil for a guide. Max Estrella is accompanied by the despicable Don Latino (note the transparently allusive name) who, instead of guiding him, confuses and deceives him, while taking advantage of his weakness. Don Latino would usually be considered "realistic," using the term as a euphemism for "ignoble."

The unexpected revitalization and bringing up to date of myths should prove that Valle's supposed system of deformation is not really so systematic and does not always produce the same effects. The destruction of the myths, or beliefs and values, on which middle class society is based does not annihilate—though it does transform—other types of myths, especially that of the poet as clairvoyant and prophet. The poet may not be a "tower of God," as Darío put it, but he does end up as a blind prophet, the chosen one, although being chosen by the Gods may be more a punishment than a prize, from the standpoint of calm and security. The intensity of revelation that distinguishes the poet from other men is accompanied by an intensity of suffering, also imposed by the Gods. Perhaps it would be relevant to recall that the unfortunate Alejandro Sawa, whose life provided the raw materials for Valle's characterization of Max Estrella, wrote a book, published posthumously, entitled *Iluminaciones en la sombra (Illuminations in the Darkness).*

Something else must be said regarding the transformation of reality into an *esperpento.* Reality is naturally not grotesque; it simply *is.* If it seems grotesque, it is because our vision qualifies it as such. A shift in attitude or point of view alters the apparent character of what we behold. Our vision, then, creates the *esperpento*, in acting as a distorting mirror. It is not in the Callejón del Gato but in Don Ramón's own vision that we can find the concave and convex mirrors which reflect the images of classical heroes. A change in the lighting or a squint of the eyes can prevent the distortion. If a tear comes between the mirror and the reflected object, what was ridiculous becomes dramatic.

The multiplicity of perspectives clearly presented in *Los cuernos de don Friolera,* a drama between a puppet show and a ballad (which act as an anticipation and a commentary respectively), shatters any Calderonian idea of honor as well as any Romantic concept of love. Valle-Inclán, like Don Estrafalario, looks upon the goings on from "the other shore." That distance is what makes him see his characters as puppets, their emotions as insignificant, the passions revealed by their behavior as comic trifles.

Visual distance is a decisive factor in the process of turning reality into an *esperpento*. From afar the individual is diminished and dehumanized. This, in turn, lets him be observed ironically, so that the onlooker does not participate in the movements and gestures which seem ridiculous or even senseless. The onlooker cannot participate in what he sees because he is incapable of distinguishing or discerning. It is by the grace of creative language that Ana de Ozores and Anna Karenina seem to be like us and to be present among us, while Doña Loreta and Lupita la Romántica simply make us laugh because they are only puppets; yet they aspire to conduct themselves like people.

The reader or spectator may see things from the viewpoint and in the perspective selected for him by the author. But he also sees—or imagines—things which the latter purposely omits. He comes to realize that to see things from the inside leads to tolerance, whereas to see them from the outside leads to criticism, distortion, and caricature. The poor cripple in Córdoba who used to be called "Engañabaldosas" (sidewalk-cheater), because when he walked he would lift his lame foot in one direction and bring it down in another, certainly saw himself quite differently from those who gave him the nickname. He was both pitiable and laughable, depending on the spiritual distance of the beholder.

If an individual who is inside accepts the view as seen by one outside, what occurs is a voluntary transformation of reality into an *esperpento*. The buffoon (admirably portrayed in Valle by characters like Nachito Veguillas and Doctor Polaco) is willing to be the muddled image in a distorting mirror. The examples are numerous in Valle's work (and in those of others: a case in point is Don Fulgencio in Unamuno's *Amor y pedagogía*). This is not surprising, for—as we have all admitted—Spanish life is itself an *esperpento*. The young men of Mondragón who in 1956 ate a donkey in homage to Juan Ramón Jiménez's Platero, and the one-eyed Spanish psychiatrist in New York who shocks his distinguished lady patients when (as if to emphasize his bewilderment at such an unusual problem) he suddenly taps his monocle against his glass eye, a replacement of the one he lost in the Spanish Civil War, are living proofs of the vitality and reality of the *esperpento.*

NOTES

[1] Cited by Georg Lukacs: *Teoría de la novela,* Editorial Siglo XX, Buenos Aires, p. 20.

[2] *Las estéticas de Valle-Inclán,* pág. 85.

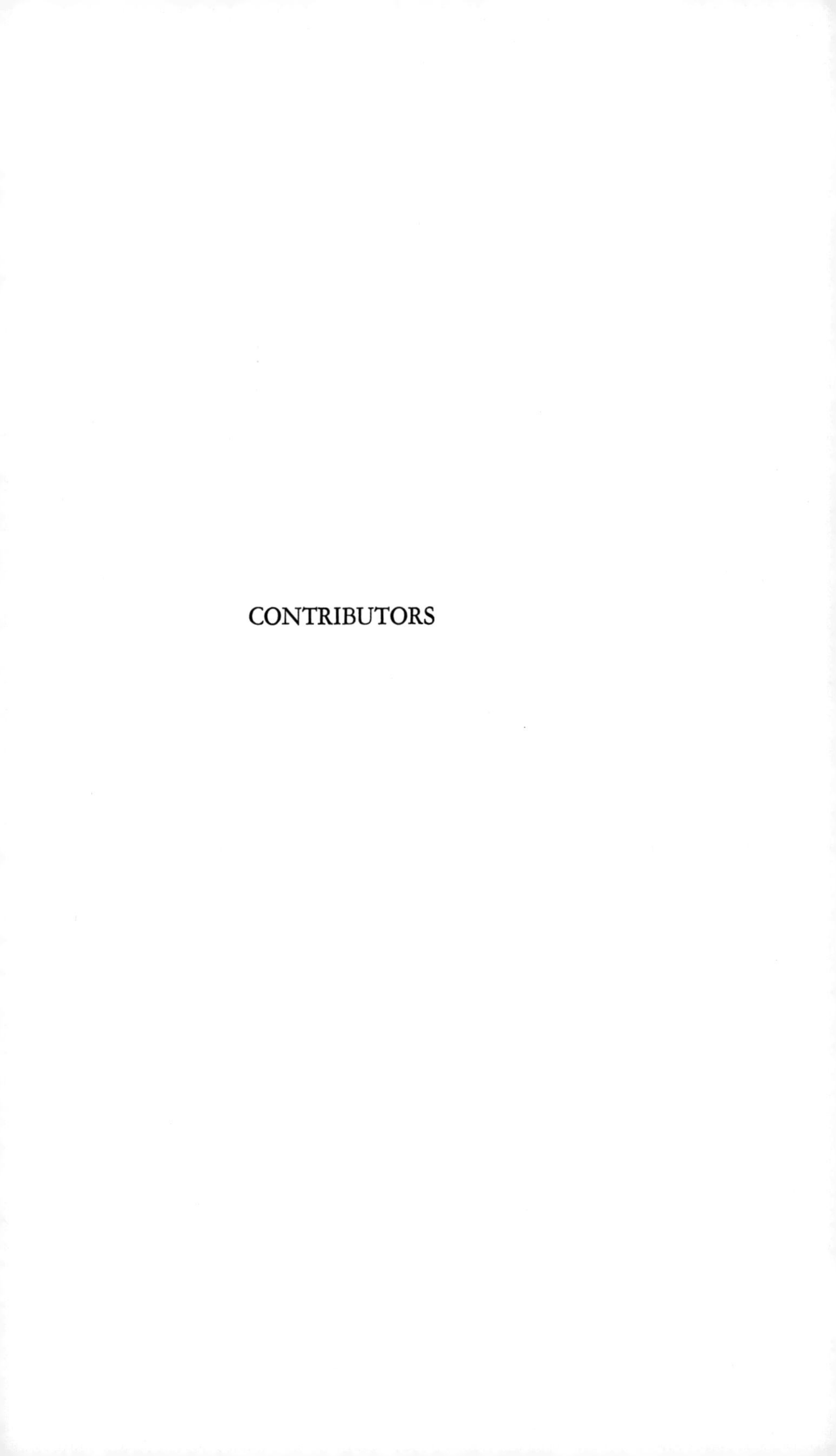

CONTRIBUTORS

RAMÓN MARTÍNEZ-LÓPEZ is Professor of Romance Languages at The University of Texas at Austin. He is editor of *Image of Spain* (a volume on its life, art and literature in the 20th century; Austin, 1961); *General Estoria: Versión Gallega del Siglo XIV* (Oviedo, 1963); *Antonio Machado, Prosas y poesías olvidadas* (with Robert Marrast; Paris, 1964); *Unamuno Centennial Studies* (Austin, 1966).

*

JOSÉ RUBIA BARCIA is Professor of Spanish and Portuguese at the University of California, Los Angeles, and Chairman of the Department. Creative writer and critic, he is the author of *A Bibliography and Iconography of Valle-Inclán, 1866–1936* (Berkeley, 1960) and *Umbral de sueños* (Los Angeles, 1961).

*

ILDEFONSO MANUEL GIL is now Professor of Spanish Literature at City University of New York (Brooklyn College). He is a novelist and critic whose works include: *La moneda en el suelo* (Barcelona, 1951); *Cancionerillo del recuerdo y la tierra* (Zaragoza, 1952); *El incurable* (Madrid, 1957); *Pueblonuevo* (Madrid, 1961), and *Los días del hombre* (Santander, 1968).

FRANCISCO AYALA is Professor of Spanish Literature at the University of Chicago. Besides a critic, Dr. Ayala is well known as a sociologist and novelist. His works include: *Historia de macacos* (Madrid, 1955); *El escritor en la sociedad de masas* (Buenos Aires, 1958); *Experiencia e invención* (Madrid, 1960); *Muertes de perro* (Buenos Aires, 1958, English translation, *Death as a Way of Life*) and El *fondo del vaso* (Buenos Aires, 1962).

*

JOSÉ LUIS CANO is a poet and critic who lives in Madrid. He is co-editor of the much-circulated journal *Insula.* Among his works are *Antología de la nueva poesía española* (Madrid, 1958); *Biografía ilustrada de Federico García Lorca* (Barcelona, 1962); *Otoño en Málaga* (Madrid 1960) and *Luz del tiempo* (Madrid 1962).

*

RICARDO GULLÓN, who edited the present volume, is Professor of Romance Languages at The University of Texas at Austin. He is the author of *Las secretas galerías de Antonio Machado* (Madrid, 1958); *Estudios sobre Juan Ramón Jiménez* (Buenos Aires, 1960); *Autobiografías de Unamuno* (Madrid, 1964); *Galdós, novelista moderno* (Madrid, 3rd edition 1966). He is presently writing a book on techniques of the novel.